MADE
COMPLETE
IN CHRIST

PEACE AMBA

authorHOUSE

AuthorHouse™
1663 Liberty Drive
Bloomington, IN 47403
www.authorhouse.com
Phone: 833-262-8899

Published by AuthorHouse 09/09/2021

ISBN: 978-1-6655-3724-7 (sc)
ISBN: 978-1-6655-3725-4 (e)

Library of Congress Control Number: 2021918133

Print information available on the last page.

Main Bible Passage

And ye are complete in him, which is the
head of all principality and power.
—Colossians 2:10

CONTENTS

THE GOD-HUMAN RELATIONSHIP

Introduction

There is more to the life of a person than the physical presence. There is, in fact, more to each human being than what we see or perceive. There is an unknown expanse that only God is privy to. Such is entirely the purview of the Creator of heaven and earth, much beyond what you and I can understand. As such, there are issues that are beyond our control as human beings. There are things beyond human comprehension, things we need the divine helper to know, do, and achieve. For any human being to deny this is to ignore the truth. The truth is that secret things belong to God; what is known is man's.

Within that unknown continuum, only God is able. Within it, he has the capacity that humans do not have. He has created that space for himself and himself alone. It is a space he wants humans to allow him to fill. Without him, it remains empty, incomplete. Meanwhile, many believe when they have one specific thing that they desire, it will lead to their fulfilment. They feel having what they desire makes them complete. They have it but realize there is still a gaping, empty space. It is a space that no man, no material thing, no level of achievement can fill. It is the space for God. Until each of us allows God to take charge of that which only he is able to, there is ever that space. It is unfilled. It is one reason so many people feel unfulfilled in spite of what they have achieved in other spheres of their lives. They have this sense of incompleteness to them, a feeling of emptiness. It is where God should be. That is how he has ordained it from the beginning. As God's workmanship, it is only when he is given the space that only he can fill that we are made complete. The Lord Jesus Christ is at the center of this divine design. In him, the divine plan is fulfilled.

The word of God makes it clear that in Jesus Christ, while on earth, God takes human form. By the time he left the earth, the word of God made it known that God has given all power to him in heaven and on earth. Jesus is above all things made. For by him, all things were made, and without him, nothing was made that was made (John 1:3). At the mention of his name, all knees must bow in heaven and on earth and under the earth. In him, God says he delights. He says all humans should hear him. Why should God say this about Jesus Christ?

God has given an instruction. He knows it is to the benefit of mankind that those divine instructions are obeyed. For every instruction God gives contains seeds that are of benefit to his workmanship. They are instructions that bring about the filling of the space that God has created for only himself in us humans. Walking in those instructions ensures that a person is never left empty, unfulfilled, or incomplete. Walking in them ensures we become the best he has purposed we should be. This is what I explain in this book. I pray that God will breathe on it, the Holy Spirit will grant you understanding, and it shall be of benefit to you in the name of Jesus.

Why God?

The answer to this question is taken for granted by many because they have the understanding that without a creator, creation cannot exist. But there are people who ask this question, and there are others who believe there is no God. As such, answers to the question have to be provided, as knowledge leads to realization, which, in turn, leads to a decision. Each of us needs to decide for God. We can do this through his son, Jesus Christ. The foremost reason is that it is for our own good as humans that we decide for God. We stand to benefit much if we do.

The God we refer to is the Creator of the world and everything that is in the world, as noted in Psalm 24:1–2, which says, "The earth is the LORD's, and the fulness thereof; the world, and they that dwell therein. For he hath founded it upon the seas, and established it upon the floods."

Contrary to the claim by some that humankind evolved from microorganisms, the Word of God says in Genesis 2:27–28 that God created man in his own image: "So God created man in his own image, in the image of God created he him; male and female created he them."

God deliberately formed man using earth, as established in Genesis 2:7, which says, "And the LORD God formed man of the dust of the ground, and breathed into his nostrils the breath of life; and man became a living soul."

The argument may continue forever, but the Word of God is the truth. God made the universe, and he put man in it. For the sake of reasoning it may be argued that if anyone must err, it should not be against what is reasonable. No house suddenly stands, except some people roll up their sleeves and build it. No home happens except two adults agree to live together in it and raise children. The wonders and products of science and technology that we take for granted these days do not suddenly come into existence. People worked on it. Our beautiful cities did not just spring into existence. People worked on them. As for our wonderful universe, where all these things take place, however, it is said in some circles that it came into existence on its own, that no one was responsible for it. The rest of that argument is beyond the scope of this book. The focus here is to state that God created humanity, and it is for the benefit of humanity that we give him the glory and worship him.

God has made human beings the masterpiece of his creation, the ultimate in all that he has made. We are God's representation on the earth. When he created humankind, his plan was that we should be rulers over all other things. Sin became a barrier between God and humans; it was not God's purpose that humans should be subjected to suffering, disease, death, and other conditions that do not glorify him. Originally, humans were made for bliss and foreverness.

For this reason, no human being is an accident on earth. God arranged for our coming long before we arrived, as stated in Jeremiah

1:5–6, which says, "Before I formed thee in the belly I knew thee; and before thou camest forth out of the womb I sanctified thee, and I ordained thee a prophet unto the nations."

Not one of us is an option. No human being is an alternative. God created you as you. He created you because he wanted to, and he has his purpose for you. You are not a mistake, not the child your parents never wanted to have. God wanted each of us to be here, and that is why we are here. How each of us came is not the issue. It is never our fault how we came. The important thing is that God released us to come into the world. If he had not, we would not be here in the first place.

As he has sent us to the earth, he has also made available all we need in order to fulfil the purpose for which we are here. Like a responsible parent, God created us, and he takes it as his duty to take care of us. Take note that in God's view, we are his children when we come to him through his son, Jesus Christ. We are a wonder of his creation, fearfully and wonderfully made, according to Psalm 139:14: "I will praise thee; for I am fearfully and wonderfully made: marvellous are thy works; and that my soul knoweth right well."

We are a people of substance, designed to show forth God's glory. We are a treasure—his treasure. He has ordained that we rule on this earth, not to be ruled by anything, as stated in Genesis 2:28. "And God blessed them, and God said unto them, Be fruitful, and multiply, and replenish the earth, and subdue it: and have dominion over the fish of the sea, and over the fowl of the air, and over every living thing that moveth upon the earth."

As God's children, we are a ministry, and each of us has a ministry. Through us, God would like to display to those who do not know him that he is God and that he rules in the affairs of people. God's children are here so that his glory might be manifested through us to our world. This is a vital aspect of God's purpose for his children. Through us he shows the world who he is. He shows what only he can do. He shows that he is king over all. In the lives of his children, he displays his power. This is so important to God. In a world where everyone ignores him, he selects people through whom he shows he is the Lord of the universe. From time to time, he raised people who would show forth his glory. In them and through them, he demonstrated that there is a God who sits in heaven and uses the earth as his footstool. We have examples in the lives of many Bible characters. Here are a few examples.

Abraham

God selected Abraham and separated him. Through Abraham, God began the process of forming a nation that would be known only by his name, a nation that would be wholly dedicated to worshipping the one and only true God. He set aside this man, and through his seed, he raised the nation of ancient Israel. In a world full of idolatry, God spoke the following to Abraham, as recorded in Genesis 12:1–4:

> Now the LORD had said unto Abram, Get thee out of thy country, and from thy kindred, and from thy father's house, unto a land that I will shew thee: And I will make of thee a great nation, and I will bless thee, and make thy name great; and thou shalt be a blessing: And I will bless them that bless thee, and curse him that curseth thee: and in thee shall all families of the earth be blessed. So Abram departed, as the LORD had spoken unto him; and Lot went with him: and Abram was seventy and five years old when he departed out of Haran.

It is significant to note that after he left the land of idol worship, he was able to devote all his attention to the worship of God. He raised an altar to the true God, as noted in Genesis 12:7. "And the LORD appeared unto Abram, and said, Unto thy seed will I give this land: and there builded he an altar unto the LORD, who appeared unto him."

God began a journey with Abraham that took centuries to become manifest. He said he would give the land of Canaan to the descendants of Abraham. One of those descendants was Jesus Christ, the Savior of the world. When God selected Abraham, he began to give him instructions one step at a time. He gave him instructions in phases. Over time, nations around took note that Abraham had a God and that he worshiped a God who was different from the idols they were worshiping. Wherever Abraham went, God fought for him. He was dreaded by whoever touched him, as shown in Genesis 20:2–3, 7:

> And Abraham said of Sarah his wife, She is my sister: and Abimelech king of Gerar sent, and took Sarah. But God came to Abimelech in a dream by night, and said to him, Behold, thou art but a dead man, for the woman which thou hast taken; for she is a man's wife … Now therefore restore the man his wife; for he is a prophet, and he shall pray for thee, and thou shalt live: and if thou restore her not, know thou that thou shalt surely die, thou, and all that are thine.

Abimelech reported what happened to him in his dream to all the members of his household. He did not know the God of heaven before then. But he did through Abraham. God manifesting himself through Abraham and on behalf of Abraham continued throughout the life of this patriarch and until the child of promise, Isaac, arrived. God's plan to have a nation that would be dedicated to him continued through Isaac also.

Isaac

Isaac grew up knowing about the God of heaven, whom his father served. In time, God revealed himself to this descendant of Abraham. Isaac had a plan to go to Egypt because there was a famine in the land. However, God had a different plan for him. He instructed Isaac on where to live in Genesis 26:1–6:

> And there was a famine in the land, beside the first famine that was in the days of Abraham. And Isaac went unto Abimelech king of the Philistines unto Gerar. And the LORD appeared unto him, and said, Go not down into Egypt; dwell in the land which I shall tell thee of: Sojourn in this land, and I will be with thee, and will bless thee; for unto thee, and unto thy seed, I will give all these countries, and I will perform the oath which

> I sware unto Abraham thy father; And I will make thy
> seed to multiply as the stars of heaven, and will give
> unto thy seed all these countries; and in thy seed shall
> all the nations of the earth be blessed; Because that
> Abraham obeyed my voice, and kept my charge, my
> commandments, my statutes, and my laws. And Isaac
> dwelt in Gerar.

Isaac stayed wherever God instructed him to, and he reaped the benefits. In the course of another famine, he was instructed the same way. As a result of his obedience, he had what many nations did not have because of the famine. Through Isaac, those who worshiped idols realized he served a living God. People who did not know the one and only God began to acknowledge him.

Joseph

In the land where Joseph was held captive, God manifested himself through him. The Bible stated what happened in the household of the idol worshiper where Joseph served in Genesis 39:1–5:

> And Joseph was brought down to Egypt; and Potiphar,
> an officer of Pharaoh, captain of the guard, an Egyptian,
> bought him of the hands of the Ishmeelites, which had
> brought him down thither. And the LORD was with
> Joseph, and he was a prosperous man; and he was in the
> house of his master the Egyptian. And his master saw
> that the LORD was with him, and that the LORD made
> all that he did to prosper in his hand. And Joseph found
> grace in his sight, and he served him: and he made him
> overseer over his house, and all that he had he put into
> his hand. And it came to pass from the time that he
> had made him overseer in his house, and over all that
> he had, that the LORD blessed the Egyptian's house for
> Joseph's sake; and the blessing of the LORD was upon all
> that he had in the house, and in the field.

When Pharaoh dreamed and God gave the interpretation to Joseph, the idol-worshiping king also acknowledged the God of heaven, according to Genesis 41:39–41:

> And Pharaoh said unto Joseph, Forasmuch as God hath shewed thee all this, there is none so discreet and wise as thou art: Thou shalt be over my house, and according unto thy word shall all my people be ruled: only in the throne will I be greater than thou. And Pharaoh said unto Joseph, See, I have set thee over all the land of Egypt."

Job

Job walked in the fear of God such that he was shown as a shining example to even the devil as recorded in Job 1:7–10:

> Now there was a day when the sons of God came to present themselves before the LORD, and Satan came also among them. And the LORD said unto Satan, Whence comest thou? Then Satan answered the LORD, and said, From going to and fro in the earth, and from walking up and down in it. And the LORD said unto Satan, Hast thou considered my servant Job, that there is none like him in the earth, a perfect and an upright man, one that feareth God, and escheweth evil? Then Satan answered the LORD, and said, Doth Job fear God for nought? Hast not thou made an hedge about him, and about his house, and about all that he hath on every side? thou hast blessed the work of his hands, and his substance is increased in the land.

The enemy did all he could, yet in this man's life, God displayed to the nations around that he could restore what was lost, according to Job 42:10–13:

And the Lord turned the captivity of Job, when he prayed for his friends: also the Lord gave Job twice as much as he had before. Then came there unto him all his brethren, and all his sisters, and all they that had been of his acquaintance before, and did eat bread with him in his house: and they bemoaned him, and comforted him over all the evil that the Lord had brought upon him: every man also gave him a piece of money, and every one an earring of gold. So the Lord blessed the latter end of Job more than his beginning: for he had fourteen thousand sheep, and six thousand camels, and a thousand yoke of oxen, and a thousand she asses. He had also seven sons and three daughters.

David

In David, God showed his power to raise a shepherd into a king. A boy in the wilderness was brought into the palace. He was pursued and harassed by a king, but throughout it all, David acknowledged that God saw him through. He survived the onslaughts because God was with him. Even as king, David continued to acknowledge that he would have amounted to nothing but for God's help. He acknowledged himself as incomplete without the God of heaven being by his side.

THE NATURE OF THE
GOD-HUMAN RELATIONSHIP

I t does speak to how strong the relationship God has with human
beings is, in that while we sin and stray, God remains committed to
the relationship. He is ever on the lookout for an opportunity to bring
us back to himself. He introduced the relationship, and he has continued
to nourish it. Here, God did not wait for mankind to come to him; he
came after us to find us and restore us to himself by sending Jesus. Of
this, the word of God states in Romans 5:8; "But God commendeth his
love toward us, in that, while we were yet sinners, Christ died for us."

It speaks to the strength of the relationship God elects to have with
mankind, that he sent his only begotten son. We do not refer to just
any other human being. The person who came to earth for the sake
of mankind is Jesus of whom the Bible says thus in Philippians 2:5–11:

> Let this mind be in you, which was also in Christ
> Jesus: Who, being in the form of God, thought it
> not robbery to be equal with God: But made himself
> of no reputation, and took upon him the form of a
> servant, and was made in the likeness of men: And
> being found in fashion as a man, he humbled himself,
> and became obedient unto death, even the death of the
> cross. Wherefore God also hath highly exalted him, and
> given him a name which is above every name: That at
> the name of Jesus every knee should bow, of things in

heaven, and things in earth, and things under the earth;
And that every tongue should confess that Jesus Christ
is Lord, to the glory of God the Father.

The fact that Jesus humbled himself and became obedient unto death, even the death of the cross in order to save mankind places emphasis on how important the God-man relationship is. It indicates to us the extent God is prepared to go to keep mankind to himself. For he cannot discard us, as no maker of anything would want or be willing to discard their precious creation, we are his workmanship, as stated in Ephesians 2:10, "For we are his workmanship, created in Christ Jesus unto good works, which God hath before ordained that we should walk in them."

Like the rest of us, after the children of God went their own way and they were taken captive in exile, God was still ready to gather them to himself. He brought them back to Judah from the land of captivity and at the same moment made a promise according to Nehemiah 1:9: "But if ye turn unto me, and keep my commandments, and do them; though there were of you cast out unto the uttermost part of the heaven, yet will I gather them from thence, and will bring them unto the place that I have chosen to set my name there."

Does it have any impact on our understanding that mankind turns away from God repeatedly, yet when we cry to him he listens? It says something about the relationship with God that again and again, when we repent, he forgives and accepts us back. The examples are many in the Bible, as in Judges 6:1–4:

> And the children of Israel did evil in the sight of the LORD: and the LORD delivered them into the hand of Midian seven years. And the hand of Midian prevailed against Israel: and because of the Midianites the children of Israel made them the dens which are in the mountains, and caves, and strong holds. And so it was, when Israel had sown, that the Midianites came up, and the Amalekites, and the children of the east, even they came up against them; And they encamped

against them, and destroyed the increase of the earth, till thou come unto Gaza, and left no sustenance for Israel, neither sheep, nor ox, nor ass.

When the children of Israel had these experiences, they repented and cried unto God. This time, he sent Gideon as their helper.

Does it make any difference to our understanding of this relationship that God keeps making mankind aware of the dangers of going our own way? He warns us all the time. He sends us warning of the consequences of turning away from him. He does this through his prophets in the Old Testament just as he continues to do today. There is one such message in Jeremiah 7:1–5:

> The word that came to Jeremiah from the LORD, saying, Stand in the gate of the LORD's house, and proclaim there this word, and say, Hear the word of the LORD, all ye of Judah, that enter in at these gates to worship the LORD. Thus saith the LORD of hosts, the God of Israel, Amend your ways and your doings, and I will cause you to dwell in this place. Trust ye not in lying words, saying, The temple of the LORD, The temple of the LORD, The temple of the LORD, are these. For if ye throughly amend your ways and your doings; if ye throughly execute judgment between a man and his neighbour.

Do we make sense of the fact that even when mankind kills the prophets that God sends, he still sends others? When human beings make light of the warnings of God, when we choose not to heed his persistent calls, he never stops sending his servants as we see several times in the book of Jeremiah. The people beat and jailed Jeremiah and other prophets, yet God did not stop sending his servants to warn of the consequences of going our own way. It is a sign of the strength of the relationship he established with mankind.

Though we go our own way, when the period of paying the price for our actions is up, God steps in and restores. It attests to the nature of the relationship. On one occasion, after his children had spent the set time in the land of slavery, he arranged to set them free. He brought the children of Israel back to Judah by making a king give the order that they should be assisted to return to their land, as recorded in Ezra 1–5:

> Now in the first year of Cyrus king of Persia, that the word of the LORD by the mouth of Jeremiah might be fulfilled, the LORD stirred up the spirit of Cyrus king of Persia, that he made a proclamation throughout all his kingdom, and put it also in writing, saying, Thus saith Cyrus king of Persia, The LORD God of heaven hath given me all the kingdoms of the earth; and he hath charged me to build him an house at Jerusalem, which is in Judah. Who is there among you of all his people? his God be with him, and let him go up to Jerusalem, which is in Judah, and build the house of the LORD God of Israel, (he is the God,) which is in Jerusalem. And whosoever remaineth in any place where he sojourneth, let the men of his place help him with silver, and with gold, and with goods, and with beasts, beside the freewill offering for the house of God that is in Jerusalem. Then rose up the chief of the fathers of Judah and Benjamin, and the priests, and the Levites, with all them whose spirit God had raised, to go up to build the house of the LORD which is in Jerusalem.

It is rare that a king takes people captive and then releases them. But God makes this happen all the time for those who return to him. He releases them from bondage and lets them occupy their own land. Does this say anything to us as to how much God cherishes his relationship with man? Yet he was not done. He had his plan for the entire human race.

GOD ADDED JESUS
TO THE BARGAIN

W hile God did all he did for mankind, as cited in the Old Testament, he was set on revealing Jesus when it was time. He had in mind the coming of Jesus into the world. For through Jesus, God made the final and ultimate sacrifice to redeem us for himself. When Jesus finally arrived, he was God with us, Emmanuel, God who came in human form to break the yoke of sin, to give life, to destroy the works of darkness, as Jesus says in John 10:10: "The thief cometh not, but for to steal, and to kill, and to destroy: I am come that they might have life, and that they might have it more abundantly."

What do we make of what happened to Jesus, who is 100 percent God and 100 percent man, in the garden at Gethsemane? Here he had a God-ordained assignment that would lead to the redemption of man. He wanted to turn away from the horror of pain, suffering, and death that were essentially part of his mission. But ultimately he yielded himself to God's will? It says much about how special the God-human relationship is that Jesus allowed God's will must be done. He knew the centrality of his role in the relationship. It was the reason he surrendered as recorded in Matthew 26:38–44:

> Then saith he unto them, My soul is exceeding sorrowful, even unto death: tarry ye here, and watch with me. And he went a little farther, and fell on his face, and prayed, saying, O my Father, if it be possible,

let this cup pass from me: nevertheless not as I will, but as thou wilt. And he cometh unto the disciples, and findeth them asleep, and saith unto Peter, What, could ye not watch with me one hour? Watch and pray, that ye enter not into temptation: the spirit indeed is willing, but the flesh is weak. He went away again the second time, and prayed, saying, O my Father, if this cup may not pass away from me, except I drink it, thy will be done. And he came and found them asleep again: for their eyes were heavy. And he left them, and went away again, and prayed the third time, saying the same words.

Does it tell us anything about the God-human relationship that Jesus died on the cross? The lamb of God was made a sacrifice so that we can be saved, be redeemed for God. Of this, Jesus says in John 15:13, "Greater love hath no man than this, that a man lay down his life for his friends."

Considering the fact that the blood of Jesus was shed on the cross, does it say anything to us about the nature of the relationship? Jesus knew this was crucial for our salvation, and he spoke about it even before it happened in Matthew 26:28: "For this is my blood of the new testament, which is shed for many for the remission of sins."

Does it mean anything to us that God did all of these through Jesus because he wanted to salvage the relationship he started in the garden of Eden? It is a relationship he is committed to and willing to do everything possible to maintain. You are the focus of the relationship. It is because of you God sent Jesus into the world.

Why Jesus Is Important in the God-Human Relationship

Why is Jesus Christ important in the relationship God established with mankind? It is an important question since there are persons who mention the name and dismissively add, "Whoever that is." There are many who say this in the public space. Others acknowledge God and dismiss Jesus. Some do not acknowledge either. There are those who say God and Jesus do not exist. All of that is in addition to the question some ask regarding who Jesus really is.

Christ Jesus was sent into the world because God loves mankind. That is the bottom line as the Bibles indicates in John 3:16: "For God so loved the world that he gave his only begotten son, that whosoever believeth in him should not perish but have everlasting life."

The focus of the coming of Jesus to earth was to save humans, to reconcile us back to God. God cherished the relationship he had established in the garden at Eden. After man had sinned, he made arrangement to restore us to the original state. This original state is the state of completeness. It is where God wants his children to be. By the coming of the Lord Jesus, this purpose is achieved.

Through Jesus, God brings man up again from his fallen state. He wants mankind to still be all that he had purposed right from the outset but which the enemy destroyed. Sin separates mankind from God. Sin creates a gulf. Jesus fills that gulf. In Jesus, mankind can be what God intended in the beginning. Through Christ, God purposes to save mankind from themselves. He wants to deliver us. He wants to bless us. All of that speaks to a relationship—a special relationship.

Why Jesus Christ Came into the World

a. To Save

The work of salvation is foremost in the purpose and plan of God for mankind. For all have sinned according to Romans 3:23–24: "For all have sinned, and come short of the glory of God; Being justified freely by his grace through the redemption that is in Christ Jesus."

Mankind became estranged from God because of sin, and there was the need to save us from the repercussions of sin. Sin is abominable to God. The consequence is death. Spiritual death requires spiritual resuscitation. Only the death and resurrection of Jesus makes it possible. His death and resurrection is the guarantee of being saved from sin.

Within this is the need to reconcile us to God. The work of reconciliation involves sacrifice. There is a sacrifice that does not happen except blood is shed. Except with blood, sin cannot be atoned for, as stated in Hebrews 9:22: "And almost all things are by the law purged with blood; and without shedding of blood is no remission."

The same point is stated that it is with blood atonement is made for sin according to Leviticus 17:11: "For the life of the flesh is in the blood: and I have given it to you upon the altar to make an atonement for your souls: for it is the blood that maketh an atonement for the soul."

Jesus is the only sacrifice pleasing and acceptable to God. He is the lamb of God. His blood was specially shed for the remission of the sin of mankind. He was the lamb God sent into the world and by which God made the once-and-for-all sacrifice for the sin of man. His blood was shed for the purpose of the remission of sin.

The work of salvation is the basis of the God-man relationship, or any relationship we want to have with God. Jesus is at the center of it. He came to save. He died to save. He resurrected in order that we might resurrect from the state of death that sin had caused. Without accepting the work of salvation Jesus has done, there is no reconciliation, no relationship with God. Without being redeemed by Christ, no human being can become a child of God. It is how God has set it, and there is no human reasoning that can alter what God has set in his word. Many claim one can approach God through different means, using different ways. But Jesus says he is the only way there is in John 14:6: "Jesus saith unto him, I am the way, the truth, and the life: no man cometh unto the Father, but by me."

As the lamb of God, it is through the blood of Jesus man's sin is atoned for. It is through him God makes right the wrong the sin in Eden did to the God-man relationship. By Jesus, he draws mankind back to himself.

b. To Deliver

There is the need to deliver man from the state of destruction in which he fell in the garden at Eden. The damage done at that point was in different forms, and it was extensive. All the negatives that human beings experience are a consequence of that great fall. Sometimes, however, there are reasons to wonder if as humans we have an understanding of the extent of the consequences of that fall. One physical illustration would be the mythical story of the opening of Pandora's box. Sin committed in the garden opened a floodgate of works of darkness against which humans continue to struggle and from which we need to be delivered.

When the sin in Eden happened, what was destroyed in the spiritual was even more than that in the physical. This is an angle we generally do not pay attention to, and it is probably the reason the damage done is little understood by man. God is spirit. When we commit sin, a lot of things are disorganized in the spiritual realm. We do not always connect the physical consequences of sin to this spiritual truth. But God does, because he is a spirit. As such, he sees things from the spiritual angle, unlike man, who mostly sees from the physical. Sin is abominable to him. He abhors the pollution that sin causes in the spiritual realm. Perhaps a question God asked will bring this point home, as seen in Jeremiah 3:1–3:

> They say, If a man put away his wife, and she go from him, and become another man's, shall he return unto her again? shall not that land be greatly polluted? but thou hast played the harlot with many lovers; yet return again to me, saith the LORD. Lift up thine eyes unto the high places, and see where thou hast not been lien with. In the ways hast thou sat for them, as the Arabian in the wilderness; and thou hast polluted the land with thy whoredoms and with thy wickedness. Therefore the showers have been withholden, and there hath been no latter rain; and thou hadst a whore's forehead, thou refusedst to be ashamed.

Here God uses the illustration of divorce, and it is apt. Why? Christ is the bridegroom, and his church is the bride. Here to put away is taken to mean divorce. When a person leaves his or her Maker and walks in sin, it is seen here as though divorce has taken place. God says if we go to join ourselves to the father of lies (sinners), and we come back to him, go again and still come back to him, it amounts to pollution of the land. This was what the children of Israel were doing. God is not talking about the physical pollution, which we actually cannot see when divorce happens. It is pollution in the spiritual. There is a pollution when people sin. God sees it even if we do not, and he abhors it.

Even in marital affairs between a man and a woman, it is obvious from the rate of divorce and remarriage that mankind does not see the pollution God is talking about. Why? The pollution God is talking about is the chaos caused in the spiritual realm when the sin of disloyalty to God or to a married partner is committed. In terms of the oath taken during marriage, this is broken when divorce happens. A marital oath is not just a physical thing; it is sealed in the spiritual. When a marriage oath is desecrated, pollution is the outcome in the spiritual. In terms of one person copulating with so many other people outside marriage, disorder is caused in the spiritual. Meanwhile, in the physical, it looks as though such an act is inconsequential, so people promote and revel in it.

God also referred to it as harlotry when we turn from him into sin, as noted in Jeremiah 3:6: "The LORD said also unto me in the days of Josiah the king, Hast thou seen that which backsliding Israel hath done? she is gone up upon every high mountain and under every green tree, and there hath played the harlot."

When sin was committed in the garden, so much evil was set loose on earth, the consequences of which humans continue to bear.

c. To Destroy the Works of Darkness

Works of darkness are apparent; darkness is all around, and Jesus has come to destroy it. It is not for nothing the Bible declares woe unto earth when Satan was thrown down from heaven. Satan and his hosts perpetrate evil wherever they turn. Regarding this, Jesus says in John 10:10: "The thief cometh not, but for to steal, and to kill, and to destroy: I am come that they might have life, and that they might have it more abundantly."

But Jesus is the ultimate power to which the devil and his agents are subjected. He says he has come so that we may have life. It indicates there is a gap to be filled in the life of whoever has not accepted Jesus as their Lord and Savior.

d. To Fulfill a Promise

Jesus is the fulfilment of the promise God made from the moment sin was committed in the garden. He said in Genesis 3:14–15,

> And the LORD God said unto the serpent, Because thou hast done this, thou art cursed above all cattle, and above every beast of the field; upon thy belly shalt thou go, and dust shalt thou eat all the days of thy life: And I will put enmity between thee and the woman, and between thy seed and her seed; it shall bruise thy head, and thou shalt bruise his heel.

Jesus is the foretold "seed" that God mentioned, and when the time was ripe, he came into the world. As such, the angel announced the good news to the world when Jesus was born in Luke 2:8–13:

> And there were in the same country shepherds abiding in the field, keeping watch over their flock by night. And, lo, the angel of the Lord came upon them, and the glory of the Lord shone round about them: and they were sore afraid. And the angel said unto them, Fear not: for, behold, I bring you good tidings of great joy, which shall be to all people. For unto you is born this day in the city of David a Saviour, which is Christ the Lord. And this shall be a sign unto you; Ye shall find the babe wrapped in swaddling clothes, lying in a manger. And suddenly there was with the angel a multitude of the heavenly host praising God, and saying.

Jesus knew he came to fulfill a promise. Sin puts mankind in the state of death. Jesus said he came that we might have life and have it more abundantly. It was to fulfil the promise God made back in Genesis. No human being is complete until he or she personally appropriates God's promise and its fulfillment as embodied in Jesus.

e. To Finish the Work God Has Begun

> God has always carried out the work of the salvation of his people. He has always made a way and rescued those who would live according to his instruction. In the Old Testament, God repeatedly gave instruction, and he said whoever followed it would come to him to dwell in heaven. Such would be saved. Examples of those he gave instruction who abided by it and who eventually made heaven were Abraham, Isaac, and Jacob. As such, God takes pride in these fathers of the faith and called himself the God of Abraham, Isaac, and Jacob. He said Abraham is his friend.

All the time, God saved his own when they called on him. The pattern has consistently been there in the Old Testament when God saved and delivered his people. He saved Abraham from his enemies. When the children of Israel were enslaved in Egypt, he brought them out through a demonstration of his power. When he sent them into exile in Babylon, he brought them back into their own land. Yet a time came when he sent Jesus to offer the perfect sacrifice. It is still part of the work he has always done for his people.

This work was continued in and through Jesus. He completed the work when he came to earth in the form of man. In Jesus, God finished the work of rescuing his own, which he has always done from the time sin was first committed in the garden. Jesus acknowledged this in John 19:30: "When Jesus therefore had received the vinegar, he said, It is finished: and he bowed his head, and gave up the ghost."

There is a work God finished in and through Jesus. That finished work needs to be personally appropriated by each of us. Otherwise, there is an unfilled gap, an incomplete job.

f. To Show Man What Is Possible

> Jesus, while he was on earth, showed what was possible for man. In him, it is demonstrated that man can live without sin. It was shown that, with the help of the Holy Spirit, man could have a perfect relationship with God. It was shown that with God helping one, it is possible not to fall into temptation. For the Bible says in James 1:12–16,

> Blessed is the man that endureth temptation: for when he is tried, he shall receive the crown of life, which the Lord hath promised to them that love him. Let no man say when he is tempted, I am tempted of God: for God cannot be tempted with evil, neither tempteth he any man: But every man is tempted, when he is drawn away of his own lust, and enticed. Then when lust hath conceived, it bringeth forth sin: and sin, when it is finished, bringeth forth death. Do not err, my beloved brethren.

Many of us have fallen into the habit of claiming that there is no one without sin. Many say no one can live in holiness. Meanwhile, people fall into every temptation because of the evil desires of their heart. The Bible tells us what we should avoid falling into when we are tempted. For God does not tempt with sin, so it is not God who makes one to fall into sin. The word of God shows here that it is possible not to fall into temptation when tempted. Jesus showed this was possible when he was in the form of man.

He equally shows that humans can live as gods on earth, as children of the most high that the devil cannot hold down in bondage. He says we can do the great works that he does as stated in John 14:12: "Verily,

verily, I say unto you, He that believeth on me, the works that I do shall he do also; and greater works than these shall he do; because I go unto my Father."

g. Opens Another Phase

Through Jesus, God takes forward his relationship with man. For it is in Christ, he perfects the redemption of mankind that he has always pursued right from the time sin happened in the garden of Eden. Thus, the coming of Jesus Christ into the world has much more significance than we often attribute to it. It is useful to take a look at a few of them. By so doing, we begin to get a glimpse of what the God-Christ-man relationship really involves, what it implies. But first, we need to understand that there is a relationship. Christ Jesus did not come to earth for the sake of coming. He came for mankind and because of mankind. He is the summation of the relationship God establishes with mankind, the relationship he wants to maintain with us forever. When we understand this, we have begun a journey. We understand the very essence of this book, and we can proceed from there.

JESUS: SUMMATION OF THE GOD-HUMAN RELATIONSHIP

In Jesus and through him, God's mind-set regarding us is summed up. For instance, God is forever ready to help us. But do we ask? Whenever humans ask for help, God offers it. In order for us to be saved, rescued, and delivered from the repercussions of sin, God sent Jesus. The Bible calls Jesus the wisdom and power of God. He is the embodiment of God's help. God sent us help even when we did not ask for help.

This falls into a pattern. God demonstrated again and again in the Bible his disposition to help us, even long before he sent Jesus into the world to save mankind. For instance, when Cain killed his brother and he was to bear the consequences, he complained, and God still helped him, according to Genesis 4:14–16:

> Behold, thou hast driven me out this day from the face of the earth; and from thy face shall I be hid; and I shall be a fugitive and a vagabond in the earth; and it shall come to pass, that every one that findeth me shall slay me. And the LORD said unto him, Therefore whosoever slayeth Cain, vengeance shall be taken on him sevenfold. And the LORD set a mark upon Cain, lest any finding him should kill him. And Cain went out from the presence of the LORD, and dwelt in the land of Nod, on the east of Eden.

When man does not ask for help and does not take note that God is with us ready to help us, God still offers it. Jacob had issues in his life as a fraudster and a fugitive. He did not know his fate, what might happen to his life. The Bible did not say he asked God for help, yet while was on the run, God came to assure him that he was there to help as recorded in Genesis 28:10–16:

> And Jacob went out from Beersheba, and went toward Haran. And he lighted upon a certain place, and tarried there all night, because the sun was set; and he took of the stones of that place, and put them for his pillows, and lay down in that place to sleep. And he dreamed, and behold a ladder set up on the earth, and the top of it reached to heaven: and behold the angels of God ascending and descending on it. And, behold, the LORD stood above it, and said, I am the LORD God of Abraham thy father, and the God of Isaac: the land whereon thou liest, to thee will I give it, and to thy seed; And thy seed shall be as the dust of the earth, and thou shalt spread abroad to the west, and to the east, and to the north, and to the south: and in thee and in thy seed shall all the families of the earth be blessed. And, behold, I am with thee, and will keep thee in all places whither thou goest, and will bring thee again into this land; for I will not leave thee, until I have done that which I have spoken to thee of. And Jacob awaked out of his sleep, and he said, Surely the LORD is in this place; and I knew it not.

It may be useful to ask why God would want to help Jacob who, it appeared, was not aware that God was keen to help him. The answers might indicate to each of us what we miss when we do not ask for help from a Creator who is willing.

Actually, what happened to Jacob is an example of what God's mind-set is regarding all human beings. He waits for us to come to him and ask for help. Even when we do not, he comes to us and prompts us to ask. He prompts us to turn to him because he is able to carry the burdens we struggle to carry. Has anyone been witnessed to about the love of God for them? It is prompting from God. Has anyone had near misses in one condition or the other (e.g., accident, illness, and so on)? It is a prompting. God does this and much more for only one reason. His love for us. It is the kind of love that is immeasurable, unconditional; none is ever like it. Jesus is the embodiment of that love. He is the summary of God's love.

God had said he loved Jacob. He preferred him to Esau, even before they were born. So he came to offer help to the person he loved. This sounds like what he does for all human beings. He loves his workmanship, and he comes to help us from ourselves. When we did not ask to be saved from our sins, God offered to save us. This shows the extent of his concern for mankind. Another reason God offered to help Jacob was because he had made a promise to Abraham. He had promised to make the patriarch's descendants a great nation.

In the third generation, God kept to his promise. He visited Jacob, basically to ensure this carrier of the promise knew the God who made a promise to his grandfather. For all mankind, the coming of Jesus into the world was also the fulfilment of the promise God made in the garden of Eden. Jesus is the summation of God's concern for us. When Jesus came to earth, he was the physical manifestation of God's preparedness to always help mankind. He was the summation of God's willingness to save. As such, he tells us to ask in his name in John 15:16: "Ye have not chosen me, but I have chosen you, and ordained you, that ye should go and bring forth fruit, and that your fruit should remain: that whatsoever ye shall ask of the Father in my name, he may give it you."

One main means of getting a glimpse of how Jesus is the summation of the relationship God establishes with man is in John 1:1–4: "In the beginning was the Word, and the Word was with God, and the Word was God. The same was in the beginning with God. All things were made by him; and without him was not any thing made that was made. In him was life; and the life was the light of men."

Aside other passages in the Bible, Jesus leaves us with an idea of what he represents in this God-human, higher-lower, divine-earthly arrangement. He was in the temple at one point. There he read a scripture, and he said in him the prophecy in the scripture was fulfilled as recorded in Luke 4:20–21: "And he closed the book, and he gave it again to the minister, and sat down. And the eyes of all them that were in the synagogue were fastened on him. And he began to say unto them, This day is this scripture fulfilled in your ears."

In Jesus, the savior that mankind had been waiting for arrived on the earth. He embodied the plan of God to redeem his workmanship. With his coming, the plan was fulfilled.

Jesus spoke about his relevance in God's plan for humans on several occasions. He made it clear that without him, no man is complete. He says he is the one who is now in charge of the latest in the God-human relationship. For all things God has placed in his hands according to Mathew 11:27: "All things are delivered unto me of my Father: and no man knoweth the Son, but the Father; neither knoweth any man the Father, save the Son, and he to whomsoever the Son will reveal him."

For man to have any hope of being redeemed, for instance, Jesus spoke symbolically about the significance of his flesh and his blood in John 6:54: "Whoso eateth my flesh, and drinketh my blood, hath eternal life; and I will raise him up at the last day."

He compared his role, his person, to bread or food, which every human being needs to eat in order to survive, in John 6:51: "I am the living bread which came down from heaven: if any man eat of this bread, he shall live for ever: and the bread that I will give is my flesh, which I will give for the life of the world."

He makes reference to his flesh and blood, which was brutalized and shed respectively in the course of paying the ultimate price for the salvation of humans, as recorded in John 6:56: "He that eateth my flesh, and drinketh my blood, dwelleth in me, and I in him."

Why is this the case? The illustration Jesus gives is an affirmation that it is through him we are reconciled to God. It emphasizes the point that he is central to whatever God would do for us as the work of his hands. Without him, no one is saved. Repeatedly, he drops hints of how each human being must be willing to accept him. He makes it known that whoever does helps himself. Whoever rejects Jesus forfeits all that God has positioned him to offer in the God-human relationship.

Jesus went about asking people to follow him. He knew he is life and he gives life to those who accept him. Many followed him as recorded in Mathew 4:18–22:

> And Jesus, walking by the sea of Galilee, saw two brethren, Simon called Peter, and Andrew his brother, casting a net into the sea: for they were fishers. And he saith unto them, Follow me, and I will make you fishers of men. And they straightway left their nets, and followed him. And going on from thence, he saw other two brethren, James the son of Zebedee, and John his brother, in a ship with Zebedee their father, mending their nets; and he called them. And they immediately left the ship and their father, and followed him.

Other people heard of his fame, and they benefitted from what God had positioned him to do in their lives, as recorded in Mathew 4:23–24:

> And Jesus went about all Galilee, teaching in their synagogues, and preaching the gospel of the kingdom, and healing all manner of sickness and all manner of disease among the people. And his fame went throughout all Syria: and they brought unto him all sick people that were taken with divers diseases and torments, and those which were possessed with devils, and those which were lunatick, and those that had the palsy; and he healed them.

This is important because we are in a world where people go through so much suffering. Jesus is waiting to do in their lives what he did while he was on earth, yet so many do not come to him. The same either do not believe in him, or they do not accept that he is the son of God. Yet Jesus is so central to any relationship anyone may think they have with God.

Meanwhile, Jesus is still doing the work for which God sent him to the earth. He still does work in the lives of those who accept him, those who are God's children, because it is the work the Father has committed into his hands to do, as he states in John 10:25, 32, and 37 and John 14:10:

> Jesus answered them, I told you, and ye believed not: the works that I do in my Father's name, they bear witness of me. Jesus answered them, Many good works have I shewed you from my Father; for which of those works do ye stone me? If I do not the works of my Father, believe me not. Believest thou not that I am in the Father, and the Father in me? the words that I speak unto you I speak not of myself: but the Father that dwelleth in me, he doeth the works.

With Jesus in us, he says in 1 John 4:4, "Ye are of God, little children, and have overcome them: because greater is he that is in you, than he that is in the world."

Jesus says he has overcome the world for those who believe in him. Such as accept him will have peace. He says in him can anyone have peace in this world full of chaos, war, and perpetual violence. Those who have him do not need to fret as those who do not know him must. For those who accept him, he says he has overcome the world, according to John 16:33: "These things I have spoken unto you, that in me ye might have peace. In the world ye shall have tribulation: but be of good cheer; I have overcome the world."

He says there is little anyone can achieve if he is not factored into the equation as stated in John 15:5: "I am the vine, ye are the branches: He that abideth in me, and I in him, the same bringeth forth much fruit: for without me ye can do nothing."

He says he is positioned to give rest to them that labor in Mathew 11:28–30: "Come unto me, all ye that labour and are heavy laden, and I will give you rest. Take my yoke upon you, and learn of me; for I am meek and lowly in heart: and ye shall find rest unto your souls. For my yoke is easy, and my burden is light."

When the Pharisees thought there was another person more important in the God-human relationship, Jesus says he is the one who is most important. He said they did not know God, but he did, as stated in John 8:55–58:

> Yet ye have not known him; but I know him: and if I should say, I know him not, I shall be a liar like unto you: but I know him, and keep his saying. Your father Abraham rejoiced to see my day: and he saw it, and was glad. Then said the Jews unto him, Thou art not yet fifty years old, and hast thou seen Abraham? Jesus said unto them, Verily, verily, I say unto you, Before Abraham was, I am.

Jesus says he is the embodiment of resurrection from death to eternal life. Whoever believes in him, he too shall live eternally, as recorded in John 11:25: "Jesus said unto her, I am the resurrection, and the life: he that believeth in me, though he were dead, yet shall he live."

Jesus does not mean physical death only and the resurrection into eternal life that follows for those who believe in him. First and foremost, he refers to spiritual death in sin and the need to be brought of out that state. Sin is death. Whoever sins is living in death, though he is physically alive. Jesus says in him whoever has been dead in sin will live again in God, and be born again, as well as have the ultimate eternal life. This is the plan of God for humans, and it is in Jesus the plan is achieved.

In Jesus is God's power summed up. At his name, all knees must bow. This is the greatest name in heaven and in earth, and all powers, principalities, rulers, and spiritual forces of evil in the heavenly realm bow to him. For after he had resurrected and was about to ascend to heaven, he says in Matthew 28:18, "And Jesus came and spake unto them, saying, All power is given unto me in heaven and in earth."

All who must claim they know God automatically belong to Jesus. As such, if anyone rejects him, he has rejected God himself. God loves mankind, and he says Jesus is his beloved son. We should hear him. Jesus says he is the shepherd, and he gives life to his sheep in John 10:11: "I am the good shepherd: the good shepherd giveth his life for the sheep."

He says his sheep know him just as his Father knows him, and he dies for the sake of the sheep in John 10:14–15: "I am the good shepherd, and know my sheep, and am known of mine. As the Father knoweth me, even so know I the Father: and I lay down my life for the sheep."

He says he is the door, and only through him can anyone enter and be saved from the consequences of sin in John 10:9: "I am the door: by me if any man enter in, he shall be saved, and shall go in and out, and find pasture."

He says he is the only shepherd there is when it is a matter of salvation. He is the door that opens for the sheep to enter. He is the shepherd for whom gatemen open, and he enters to take care of his sheep. He calls his sheep, and they follow him; they do not follow strangers, according to John 10:1–5:

> Verily, verily, I say unto you, He that entereth not by the door into the sheepfold, but climbeth up some other way, the same is a thief and a robber. But he that entereth in by the door is the shepherd of the sheep. To him the porter openeth; and the sheep hear his voice: and he calleth his own sheep by name, and leadeth them out. And when he putteth forth his own sheep, he goeth before them, and the sheep follow him: for they know his voice. And a stranger will they not follow, but will flee from him: for they know not the voice of strangers.

After his death and resurrection, he came to Peter and instructed him to take care of his sheep, as recorded in John 21:16–17:

> He saith to him again the second time, Simon, son of Jonas, lovest thou me? He saith unto him, Yea, Lord; thou knowest that I love thee. He saith unto him, Feed my sheep. He saith unto him the third time, Simon, son of Jonas, lovest thou me? Peter was grieved because he said unto him the third time, Lovest thou me? And he said unto him, Lord, thou knowest all things; thou knowest that I love thee. Jesus saith unto him, Feed my sheep.

As Jesus stated of himself, so have we attested to his Lordship and the fact that he is our shepherd. David says this in Psalm 24:1–3: "The LORD is my shepherd; I shall not want. He maketh me to lie down in green pastures: he leadeth me beside the still waters. He restoreth my soul: he leadeth me in the paths of righteousness for his name's sake."

The foregoing explains the centrality of Jesus in the God–human relationship. Without him in the life of any human, a supposed relationship with God is not complete. Without him in the life of any human, the person is not complete.

WHAT GOD'S CHILDREN MEAN TO HIM

This is the same as saying what you and I mean to God, how God sees us. It is important to examine this. It is important to know because many of us do not know our worth in God. We do not consider God's mind-set regarding us, and this often affects how we conduct ourselves. It is the reason many of us do what we do, say what we say, and sometimes turn away from him to go into things we should not even dare as children of God.

What Are We to God?

We are precious to Him.

All that God has done to ensure we are redeemed speaks to what we mean to him. We are his precious little children. As such, he does all that is possible to save us and keep us. For instance, he has done all he did in regard to the work of salvation for us, not for himself. In this, God demonstrates unconditional love that only he is capable of. In all that he does concerning us, he shows what we mean to him.

We are his creatures made for a purpose

We are God's workmanship, and he created us for a reason. As we are his children, he has his purpose for us. So each of us is an embodiment of a plan. This plan when fulfilled leads to the achievement of purpose, and God's plan needs to be revealed. It needs to be made manifest. This is one reason he does everything possible to keep us to himself and keep us safe. For when his purpose is achieved in us and through us, God himself is made manifest, glorified.

There was a purpose when Lazarus died, and Jesus did not get there until four days after. He wants this occurrence to be a means by which God is glorified, his power made manifest among humans. Jesus wanted those who did not believe to see the wonders of God and believe, as he said to his disciples in John 11:4–15: "Then said Jesus unto them plainly, Lazarus is dead. And I am glad for your sakes that I was not there, to the intent ye may believe; nevertheless let us go unto him."

In all his creation, God wants to be glorified. This is more so where human beings are concerned. He has made us to be above all other things he created. As such, in humans, you and I, God is glorified more than in any of his other works of creation. For he made us in his own image and put in us his own breath, according to Genesis 2:7: "And the Lord God formed man of the dust of the ground, and breathed into his nostrils the breath of life; and man became a living soul."

He gives us dominion above every other thing he created, as recorded in 1:26–28:

> And God said, Let us make man in our image, after our likeness: and let them have dominion over the fish of the sea, and over the fowl of the air, and over the cattle, and over all the earth, and over every creeping thing that creepeth upon the earth. So God created man in his own image, in the image of God created he him; male and female created he them. And God blessed them, and God said unto them, Be fruitful, and multiply, and replenish the earth, and subdue it: and have dominion over the fish of the sea, and over the fowl of the air, and over every living thing that moveth upon the earth.

You and I are not an accident. God's children are not an accident on earth. Even when parents claim we are the children they did not plan to have, the believer is purposely sent. It is just that those who say a child is an accident do not know it. God has created each of us from eternity to function in time. The coming of each us to this earth was arranged before we arrived, as noted in Jeremiah 1:5–6: "Before I formed thee in the belly I knew thee; and before thou camest forth out of the womb I sanctified thee, and I ordained thee a prophet unto the nations. Then said I, Ah, Lord GOD! behold, I cannot speak: for I am a child."

We are not an option. We are purposely formed. We are not void. Never empty. As God's children we are not useless, and if that is what anyone says, we must never believe him or her. We must believe his word concerning us instead. For it is God's word that matters. All other things can be a lie. God's word is never a lie. What he says we are is what we are. We need to know who we are in him. When we realize who and what we are, no devil can get us confused. We will not take the wrong route and go astray. What humans around us say will not confuse us. What our situation is physically is not what matters. It may be the fact, but it is not the truth. Jesus is the truth. What he says we are is the truth in spite of the unenviable situation we may find ourselves in. What God has made us to be as his children is what counts. It is what we need to ensure we manifest. We will manifest what God makes us to be in the name of Jesus.

No child of God is void. We are not a void. We are not empty. We are heavily endowed, greatly anointed for the manifestation of his wonders. As believers, we are people of substance. The world may not see it, but God does. If we see what he sees with the eyes of faith, we will manifest it. It is how this thing works. He knows what he has designed his children for. We are his wonder, fearfully and wonderfully made. He designed us to display his wonder. When we do, people wonder. They wonder at the kind of God he is. They wonder at the kind of person he has made us to be. They wonder at the kind of God we serve. God's children are a wonder of creation, the best God has to offer. No child of his is an accident. God who created us did not make a mistake. He has not committed an error. He has his plan, and it will be manifest in our lives in the name of Jesus.

We are a treasure. God made his children a treasure, his treasure, as stated in 2 Corinthians 4:7: "But we have this treasure in earthen vessels, that the excellency of the power may be of God, and not of us."

The children of God are precious to him. He says as a mother does not forget the child in her arms, so he does not forget his children. God says even if a mother does forget, he does not forget. That is what God's children mean to him.

We are a ministry. We have a ministry. We are not a "common generality." We are more than what circumstances at the moment may say. In fact, when God does what only he can do in us, the same circumstances minister to others, and his name is thereby glorified.

We are God's representatives on earth.

As God's creation, we are his representatives on earth. As we are his children through our faith in Jesus, what we do on earth is what he does. The names the first man gave to God's creation, the animals, were what they were. As believers what we decree is what he decrees. What we say should happen is what shall happen. When we ask him for the heathens, he says he will give them to us (Psalm 2:8), and in all these, he makes himself manifest to others who do not know him yet. In us and through us, he wants the world to know that he is the King of kings and the Lord of lords. Jesus says whatever we bind on earth shall be bound in heaven and what we loose shall be loosed in heaven also. This is what God's children mean to him, his representatives on the earth.

God's plan and purpose regarding this fully come into manifestation when we live according to his will, when we walk as he instructs, when we accept Jesus who redeems us from our sins. He has made the earth for us. He has given us dominion in it. What he gives he does not take, except the receiver chooses to not walk in a way that ensures what has been deposited in him becomes manifest. From God's perspective, he made us to represent him and thereby to shine forth his glory. In doing this, we also become what he has planned that we should be. That is what God's children mean to him.

Christ and You

It is pertinent to round off this segment by properly establishing the relationship there is between Christ Jesus and you. Why? Salvation is a personal thing. If you get the point of the relevance of Jesus in your life, and you have him, you are covered. The expression "Life without Christ is a life of crisis" is a familiar one. The world is in crisis because Christ has been largely taken out of the picture. In the face of what is referred to as civilization, modernity, mankind increasingly depends on their own strength, their knowledge, or their ability. On the strength of what science says, God and his word are overlooked. He has been taken out of the equation. Yet this is the same Christ by whom and for whom the world is created. Nothing is made that is made without him. All power is given to him in heaven and in earth. The Bible says God rules in the affairs of men. He sits in heaven, and he uses the earth as his footstool. It is this same God, most people in our world pay no attention. And they lead others away from God as well.

However, when we imagine a car that develops problems, but its maker or a person who has a knowledge of how the car works is not invited to solve the problems, then we begin to get an idea of what is happening in our world. The one who is able to fix our world is no longer reckoned with. When individuals leave out of their affairs the God whose workmanship they are, then no one needs to wonder why the lives of many are full of crises.

Yet God created us, and he is able to fix us up. This is done in and through Christ Jesus. When you have him, you have all. When Christ is your Lord and Savior, you are in safe hands. You are covered. For he is able to do what no man can do. He is the ultimate fixer. He fills those empty spaces in you. He is the completeness you need, the completeness you have been looking for. Only he can do it like no other.

When Jesus is in charge of your life, he leaves nothing untouched. He takes care of what is seen and unseen about you and your circumstances. This is where Christ is crucial. Here is where he is a factor that you and I cannot afford to overlook. For there is what only he can do. We refer to the same Christ Jesus who says "without me ye can do nothing."

Nonetheless, there is a need to take a closer look at the place of Christ Jesus in our relationship with God. For instance, when we say we as humans are made complete in Christ, we can ask, "What do we mean? How?" There is also the need to see what we stand to benefit when we are in Christ, even as there are aspects of the relationship that we must fulfill in order to access the benefits. These are explained in subsequent chapters.

MADE COMPLETE IN CHRIST: WHAT DOES IT MEAN?

God made us complete in his son and through his son. Therefore, when we have Christ Jesus as our Lord and Savior, we are complete. For in him we access the grace God has placed in his son. In fact, Jesus is the grace of God. He embodies the grace of God for humans. Why does Jesus matter? Why are we made complete only in him and through him?

The Bible says God looked at everything he created in the beginning, and he saw it was good. Mankind was good. He was without sin. He had perfect fellowship with God. But there was the story of the fall of man that followed. In Jesus, mankind is redeemed. We become what God created us to be at the outset. He restored man to the state he had in the beginning. Without this restoration, no human being is complete. That is how crucial Jesus is. How does Jesus play this part, and in what other ways does he play a part in the God–human relationship? This is explored below.

The Place of Christ Jesus

By him, all things were made.

Jesus was not a new phenomenon who suddenly came on the scene when he was born. He was there in the beginning when God created the heavens and the earth. The Bible says all things that were made were made by him, and in him, all things consist. When human beings believe him and surrender to him, they have simply surrendered themselves to their creator, the power by whom and for whom all things were made. They turn themselves over to the one who knows them. They return to the porter's shed to be reshaped, rejigged, and reinvigorated for the race that we must all run. They have come back to the one who knows every part of his workmanship and knows it only too well.

The other side to this is that when human beings choose not to come to Jesus, they have missed out on what the creator has to offer.

He is the way.

No one embarks on a journey without an idea of how to get to the destination. When one sets out without an idea of which route to take, then something is missing. The information needed for a successful outing is not complete.

When people know the way to where they are going, it removes so many false starts, unnecessary hassles, failures, disappointments, and frustrations. Jesus is the way, and he has said so (John 10:10). For the way to destiny is known best to the destiny maker. He knows the best route, short or long. Many ignore the role of God in their lives and miss it in a big way. For the Bible says there is a way that seems right to a man, but the end thereof is destruction.

Jesus is the way to God. He is the way to heaven. He is the one by whom he saves the world. He says if anyone believes in him, though the person dies, he or she shall live.

He is the truth

Jesus is the truth. What he says concerning God is the truth. What he says concerning those who believe in him is the truth. There is a truth regarding every person. What happens around the person that does not align with God's word is not the truth. The plan that God has concerning his children is the truth. Anything different is not. Jesus says he is the only way to God, and that is the only truth. What he says those who believe in him should do is the truth. What he says is the right path to a destination is the truth. The way he has set to get there is the truth. Any other way is a lie, and it cannot lead to the same destination. The truth about each person—role, purpose, plan, and so on—is in God's hand. In Jesus and through Jesus, it can be manifest.

He is the life

The true life is one lived in Jesus. The Bible describes anyone outside Christ as dead. They are dead in sin. When a man said he wanted to go and bury a person, Jesus said he should follow him and let the dead bury their dead. In a spiritual sense, the person who is not in Christ is the walking dead. He or she is dead spiritually, and the ultimate eternal death still awaits. Jesus is life. In him is life. Whoever is in him is alive both spiritually and physically. Yet eternal life awaits such.

He is the resurrection and the life

In Jesus only does mankind have the hope of resurrection. In him, the person dead in sin but who repents is made alive again. In him only do the physically dead have the hope of being raised. Jesus says he is the resurrection and the life. Without resurrection, a human being forfeits an essential provision God has made. He or she is incomplete.

He is the healer

Many suffer from all manner of diseases. Yet Jesus, the divine healer, waits for them to call on him. The Bible says in 1 Peter 2:24, "Who his own self bare our sins in his own body on the tree, that we, being dead to sins, should live unto righteousness: by whose stripes ye were healed."

There is healing of all manner of ailments in Christ. Yet many succumb to ailments. The Bible says at the name of Jesus every knee shall bow. At his name, diseases bow. Illnesses disappear, and terminal diseases go. In him, the grace to be healed consists. He is the grace by which we get healed no matter what the matter is. When a person fails to have him, they miss out of the grace and the virtue that flow from him to effect healing.

Many do not have access to him, so they live as invalids. They may have all other things in material terms, but without sound health, they are incomplete. There are several examples in the Bible of people whom Jesus healed. People still enjoy the same healing power that is in the name of Jesus to this day. Whatever the ailment many be—physical, marital, financial, emotional—Jesus heals. He makes complete.

He is the Alpha and the Omega

Jesus is the beginning and the ending of everything. He knows the end from the beginning. He is the beginning and the ending of every human being. Yet the majority of people stay away from him. His absence in the life of any human being is a sign of incompleteness. When he is present, he guides, leads, protects, and provides for the person from the beginning of his or her life to the end.

He is the Messiah

Jesus is the one who has come as the Messiah, and there is no other apart from him. He has come to save the unsaved. He comes to save us from lives of many challenges and problems. He comes to rescue the perishing, raise the ill, restore hope to the hopeless, and give joy to the sad. In a world that knows nothing but chaos and despair, the Messiah comes to save those who turn to him.

He is the Prince of peace

The world cannot be without trouble; the Bible says so. It is because humans cause troubles through greed and wickedness. The world cannot change if mankind does not change. We cannot change if we do not factor Jesus into the equation. He is the Prince of peace. In the midst of all the trouble, Jesus gives peace. He gives his own people peace. Of him, the Bible says in Isaiah 9:6, "For unto us a child is born, unto us a son is given: and the government shall be upon his shoulder: and his name shall be called Wonderful, Counselors, The mighty God, The everlasting Father, The Prince of Peace."

Jesus says even those who believe in him will face tribulation, but they should be of good cheer, as he has overcome the world. Jesus is the peace the world needs. Wherever he is accepted, he brings peace and calm to turbulent situations.

All power is given to him

Jesus is the ultimate power in heaven and in earth. The Bible says all power is given unto him in heaven and in earth. All principalities and powers are under his feet. Whatever power may trouble any person, Jesus is above it, and he can bring it to submission. The person who is oppressed by anything, physical or spiritual, is not complete. But Jesus can set the oppressed free.

He is the word

By the word, the world was created. Jesus is the word. He is the ultimate word. In all things, he is the first and the last word. What he says must stand. What he orders must come to pass. The Bible says all things will pass away, but not a jot of the word of God will pass unfulfilled. When the word that is above every other word is in a person, it is complete. Nothing the enemy does can overcome him or her. Nothing the enemy says can override what God has said. His word stands sure. For he is the only foundation there is, as the word of God says in 1 Corinthians 3:11;

"For other foundation can no man lay than that is laid, which is Jesus Christ."

He is the light of the world

Jesus is the light. But the world is full of darkness because the work of the hands of mankind is the work of darkness. His thought is continually evil. The light of the world is Jesus as he says in John 8:12; "Then spake Jesus again unto them, saying, I am the light of the world: he that followeth me shall not walk in darkness, but shall have the light of life."

43

Whoever has Jesus has the light in him. The person is light. How do we know this? When we have Jesus, we come to the realization that we are different. We belong to a different class in God's creation, even among fellow humans. As such, he says we are the light of the world.

HOW DO WE KNOW WE

Are Made Complete in Christ?
Forever, O Lord, your word is settled in heaven.
—Psalm 119:89

God Is the Word; the Word Is God

God promised us so much in the Bible, and he himself is the very promise he has made. He utters words, and he is the word he utters, according to John 1:1: "In the beginning was the word and the word was with God, and the word of God."

God says a thing, and he does what he says. He is what he says. His word is immutable. He promises, and through his spirit, he goes into action and fulfils the promise. He depends on no one else to carry out what he says. So there can be no failure. A case of one person promising while the other person who should fulfill it fails does not exist where God is concerned. He says the word, and he is at the same time the doer of his word.

He Has Sworn by Himself

Perhaps one challenge that we have as humans is that we do not comprehend it when God says he swears by himself. He said so to Abraham. Yet we hardly have an understanding of what God means by that, or the extent to which he has searched and could not find anything more reassuring than himself. There cannot be anything or anyone greater than the one who creates all things in the first place. That is how immense it is when God says he has sworn by himself. When we get a hint of the full implication of this, we will then realize that in no other power can we have our completeness but God.

The Word Became Flesh

The same word was born into the world—Jesus Christ. He came in human form. He related with mankind, and he experienced what it meant to be human. Therefore, he understands what we pass through. He knows our weaknesses. He suffered what we consider suffering. He identifies with us, has compassion on us, and is ready to help us. He comes in and complements us, comforts us, and upholds us no matter what we are passing through.

He Finished the Work of Salvation on the Cross

The work of salvation was completed on the cross. He finished all that had to be done in order to reconcile man to God. While he was on the cross(John 19:30),

> "When Jesus therefore had received the vinegar, he said, It is finished: and he bowed his head, and gave up the ghost."

There is no other person who has offered himself as a sacrifice for the sin of man as Jesus did on the cross. Jesus is the ultimate sacrifice. In him and by his blood, we have remission of sin. In him, we are saved. In him, God takes pleasure in us and does all he has in mind for us. In him, he does for us what only he can do as the Creator.

Jesus Is the Embodiment of Fullness

Jesus is the embodiment of fullness, and so in him, we have fullness, as stated in John 1:16: "And of his fullness have all we received, and grace for grace."

This fullness cancels the limitations of man. It removes hindrance. It helps us to do what we have no power of our own to do. His fullness makes us full in whatever area we may experience a void. Only Jesus can do it. When we have him, we are made full, complete.

He Is the Complete Package of Impartation to Live a Glorious Life

We can be imparted to live a glorious life in him. He is the complete package of impartation for every aspect of our life. The Bible says this of Jesus in Colossians 2:9, "For in him dwelleth all the fulness of the Godhead bodily."

Whatever it is that is good that we want to experience, it is in him to do it. For who he is, is what he does. And who he is has been described to us in Isaiah 9:6–7:

> For unto us a child is born, unto us a son is given: and the government shall be upon his shoulder: and his name shall be called Wonderful, Counselors, The mighty God, The everlasting Father, The Prince of Peace. Of the increase of his government and peace there shall be no end, upon the throne of David, and upon his kingdom, to order it, and to establish it with judgment and with justice from henceforth even for ever. The zeal of the LORD of hosts will perform this.

He Is above All Principalities and Powers

Jesus sits atop all principalities and powers. He has dominion over them. They must bow to his command and wishes. The Bible says at the name of Jesus every knee shall bow, in heaven and on and under the earth.

There is no power greater than Jesus. When we have him, therefore, we are made complete. Of him, the Bible says in Acts 10:38, "How God anointed Jesus of Nazareth with the Holy Ghost and with power: who went about doing good, and healing all that were oppressed of the devil; for God was with him."

He Lives Forever

He who lives forever knows all and is above all. He knows the beginning from the beginning. He knows the end from the beginning. The Bible says in Hebrews 13:8, "Jesus Christ the same yesterday, and today, and forever."

The same Jesus who lives forever has therefore done the following concerning us.

He Predestines

The one who can predestine must be one who knows all about the other person. He is not mortal himself but immortal. He knows us before we know ourselves, even before we were born. Only Jesus answers to that. He is as such able to determine our beginning and our ending. He is able to make available what is needed for us to pass through all the stages from the beginning to the end. Of him, the Bible says in Romans 8:29–30,

> For whom he did foreknow, he also did predestinate to
> be conformed to the image of his Son, that he might be
> the firstborn among many brethren. Moreover whom

> he did predestinate, them he also called: and whom he
> called, them he also justified: and whom he justified,
> them he also glorified.

Predestination means that God has determined whatever must happen even long before it happened. Each human being was determined by God and uniquely made. This must be the reason there are billions of people on earth, but the fingerprint of one person is never the same as that of another person.

The fact that only God predestines is also stated in Ephesians 1:11, "Also we have obtained an inheritance, having been predestined according to His purpose who works all things after the counsel of His will."

When God does this, he only can lead us into fulfilling the purpose for which he created us. No other power can. It is worth noting that Apostle Paul explains that predestination happens according to God's purpose. He says God works all things, including us, after the counsel of his will.

He Calls

Jesus says no one can come to him except God makes the person to come. The Bible also says in Ephesians 2:8–9, "For by grace are ye saved through faith; and that not of yourselves: it is the gift of God: Not of works, lest any man should boast."

God calls us. This is a mystery about salvation. A person hears the word, and he or she believes and responds to it, giving his or her life to Christ. But Jesus says the person does not come of his own will. God has decided he would come. Salvation is not of a person's will but of the mercy of God to make him accept the offer of salvation. God called those he wanted. He brings such to himself by his grace. This idea of calling and being called is illustrated when Jesus talks about his sheep. He says he is the shepherd; he calls, and his sheep hear him. He says he knows his sheep, and his sheep know him. They listen to him; they do not listen to any other.

There are those called, and because they are predestined, they answer the call. He also says no one comes to him except God draws him or her. There is a measure of assurance in this for anyone that the one who calls is able to take care of all that concerns those he has called. In him, they can be made complete. This is because being called here is not just about saying, "Come." It also has to do with what God wants to do in the lives of those he calls and who respond. The call is from he who has the power to make what is dead alive again. He makes what is not to be, and he, according to Romans 4:17, "gives life to the dead and calls things that are not as though they were."

God can act creatively regarding those he calls and who respond. He can take out of darkness into light. He can take out of confusion into clarity. He has, as stated in 1 Peter 2:9, "called you out of darkness into his wonderful light."

He calls us as "a chosen people, a royal priesthood, a holy nation, a people belonging to God."

He Justifies

Justification means to set something right, or to declare righteous. In regard to this, the Bible says in Romans 8:30, "Those he predestined, he also called; those he called, he also justified."

Justification is the determined purpose of God to take sinners who have accepted Jesus as though they have never sinned. Through Jesus, God regards everyone who believes his son as justified to be his children too. Justification is beyond pardon. It is completely overlooking what the sinner has done. The sins are blotted out, forgotten in God's sight. Jesus, through his death and resurrection for the sin of all people, is the basis of this. Jesus has taken the place of sinners and has died for their sins. He has suffered the consequences of sin committed by mankind, and we do not have to suffer and die as a result of these sins. He has paid the price. He has justified us in the sight of God.

He Glorifies

Through Jesus, we shall be glorified. The idea of glorification is about the ultimate perfection of believers. It is not here. It happens in the hereafter, and the fact that Jesus lives is the guarantee believers will be glorified. Glorification is where believers are headed. It is actually the goal of believers when God effectually called and regenerated us. The doctrine of glorification is about being done with sin and instead dwelling in the presence of God.

Glorification is done without the contribution of the believer. He or she believes and on the basis of his or her confession is a candidate for glorification acquired at the expense of Christ.

HOW DOES CHRIST MAKE COMPLETE?

He Redeems

The work of redemption is the single most important work Jesus does through his death and resurrection. The word implies that something or someone is lost, gone astray, but is found and restored back to the owner, to the original state. This is the condition of every human being who has not accepted Jesus as his or her personal Lord and Savior. This has been the situation since the time the first man sinned in the garden. Therefore, we must be redeemed from sin. We must be redeemed from the rightful hold the devil has on man since the great disobedience happened in the garden of Eden.

Every human being has to be redeemed by God and for God. Without redemption, there is no sonship. Without the redemption power in the death and resurrection, no human being can be a child of God. It is in Jesus and by him the work of redemption is achieved and completed in the life of every believer.

He Gives Victory

A life of victory over obstacles is not automatic. It is by the grace of God. He gives the grace to whomever he wishes. Life is full of obstacles, human, non-human, spiritual. Actually, what many rationalize as a medical condition and give all manner of strange medical terms may be spiritually induced, an attack from the pit of hell. It is Jesus who has triumphed over hell, and only he can make us triumph over evil machinations that come in the form of diseases, disabilities, and so on.

Victory comes from God. Healing is from God. There are human obstacles so powerful that it is only at the name of Jesus they bow. An example will suffice. What can a citizen do when an authoritarian head of state decides he must be executed. There was a well-known servant of God who said a head of state had scheduled that he be arrested and possibly killed. The man of God turned to God. Before the instruction could be executed, the head of state was dead. Victory belongs to God. Forces of wickedness that operate in the world of the unseen are comparable to the vindictive head of state. Only through Jesus can we truly overcome them.

Wherever we turn, it is impossible to live a worthwhile life without being victorious always. There will always be challenges, and they must be overcome. Every inch of the way is littered with obstacles, with barriers—spiritual, physical, financial. No one can say they are complete when they fall at the slightest attack every now and then. Sickness, terminal diseases, mental illness, addiction to drugs and other dangerous substances, lack of progress, fruitlessness, wayward children, barrenness—the list is endless. These are obstacles. Only God gives victory, and no human being is complete until he or she has the God-kind of victory over obstacles that come his or her way.

He Delivers

Deliverance is the meat of the children of God; Jesus said so. God is the only deliverer. No one else can deliver. True deliverance cannot happen through any other power except Jesus. Actually, when people have issues, and they approach what has no power, what they do is make appeasement to demons and witches and the rest of them. They do not deliver. They appease. There is a price to this. The person on behalf of whom appeasement is made is still subject to those who have been appeased, and they can strike anytime they wish. Whoever seeks deliverance this way is an enemy of God, and they cannot make heaven.

Jesus is the true deliverer. When he delivers, he does it completely. He can deliver from any bondage the devil may have put a human being into, and no one can question him. For he is above all principalities, powers, and rulers, and all spiritual forces of evil in the heavenly realms.

There are issues for which every human being needs deliverance. When we have it, and have it from Jesus Christ, we are complete. There are a lot of issues that people treat using experts. All they need is a word from the Lord Jesus, and they are completely free from whatever it is. What they need to do is call on Jesus, and he will set them free. The daughter of the Gentile woman needed deliverance. She only got it when Jesus sent a word to her.

The child of the Roman centurion needed deliverance. It was done when Jesus stepped into his matter.

The woman with the issue of blood needed deliverance. She touched the hem of the garment of Jesus, and she was delivered. She was made complete.

He Strengthens

God says in his word, "I will strengthen him, I will help him, and I will uphold him with my hand of righteousness" (Isaiah 41:10). What man does not need God does not offer. He does not promise it. His promises were there before mankind was created. God made the promises because he knew that along the way every man would need him. He promises to strengthen because we need to be strengthened. We are too weak to go all the way by ourselves. Jesus says without him, we can do nothing. We are not complete until he steps in and helps. He promised to send the comforter. It is because we need the comforter. He strengthens us when we cannot help ourselves. It is when he does that we are made complete.

He Fights for Us

Whether anyone believes it or not is not the issue. The fact is that the natural man is confronted on all fronts with battles both spiritual and physical. The emotional battles are as destructive as the marital, mental, financial, or health-related battles. The statistics in each country speak to this fact. Crime wastes lives as drug abuse, depression, or suicide wastes lives. Human solutions are proffered, but things often appear to get worse. The facts and figures speak to that too. It means we confront battles that are way beyond human capacity. Without God's capacity coming into the picture, there is a gap that remains to be filled. There is that incompleteness that we need to make up for.

The children of Israel knew this, so each time they came up against a battle, they cried to God for help. And he did help. Sometimes they did not even have to pick up a weapon. All the weapon they needed was singing praise to God. They did at the wall of Jericho, and it came down. On some other occasions, a battle they dismissed as small soon became a nightmare for them. The battle against the city of Ai is an example. The children of Israel thought the city was small, and it was there for them to take. They were defeated. How many battles do humans consider little problems, and then they turn out to be insurmountable? We see them in world—those battles in which even experts' solutions have failed.

These days, there is that dependence on human knowledge when we confront many of the battles as communities and as individuals. Human knowledge is good. God gave it. Yet this God equally warns his workmanship not to forget him or depend on their own strength or knowledge. This is why the word of God says the race is not to the swift, nor the battle to the strong.

There are battles that on our own we cannot win. If that were not the case, Moses would not have asked God for his presence in the course of the journey to the Promised Land. Moses knew it was with God the journey through the wilderness would be complete. Without God, they were on their own, and they would be overrun by all manner of enemies. The enemies we confront are too many for us. The battles are too strong for us to want to fight them on our own. When God fights for his children, he wins for them.

He Blesses

God blesses. We all need the God-kind of blessing. No person is complete without it. With God's blessing in our lives, we will not struggle with most of the issues that people struggle with. Why? God's blessing has unique characteristics; the Bible says the blessing of God brings wealth, and he adds no sorrow.

There is nothing comparable to God's blessing. When he blesses, it is complete. He does not leave an aspect. Rather it is an all-around blessing. God will not bless a person with financial resources and leave him or her in ill health. He would not bless with materials things and then cut short the life of the same person. He will not give money and leave problem children for us to struggle with. That is not a complete blessing. Only God gives a blessing that is complete.

God will not bring his children into a marriage that they endure rather than enjoy. When he blesses with a spouse, it is a person who loves him and loves his child. His blessing lifts from glory to glory. His blessing is not up today and down tomorrow. His blessing does not rely on how well the stocks are doing. It has nothing to do with the well-being of the economy. In fact, his blessing shines forth and glorifies him when there is economic meltdown. This is attested to when Isaac sowed during a famine and reaped a hundredfold.

God knows what we need, and he is there to supply more than enough. So God's word says in Hebrew 13:5, "Let your conversation be without covetousness; and be content with such things as ye have: for he hath said, I will never leave thee, nor forsake thee."

He Heals

God heals. Illness is not only physical; it is spiritual, emotional, financial, and marital. God heals all. He leaves none untouched. When he heals, it is comprehensive. What is not comprehensive is not complete, and this is the nature of every human-driven solution. We can see it around us. As much as mankind tries to find solutions to heal many of the ailments plaguing the universe, it does not seem like they bring about the permanent results expected. Individuals search for a permanent solution that they can hardly get from human effort. But only God offers what is permanent. He does what is complete.

No one is truly healed until they are made whole. Wholeness implies a complete package. Only God gives the complete package. What many get is that they may be healed of a sickness physically, but they are not healed emotionally. They may be stable financially, but they are not stable mentally. Their marriage may be stable, but they are not healed in fruitfulness or prosperity. That is not God's wish for anyone who belongs to him. God does not just heal; he makes whole.

Many may be healed of an illness, but sometimes there is a relapse. They are constant faces in clinics and hospitals around the world. Most famous physicians and surgeons around the world know them and make money out of them. Some are financially fine today, but tomorrow they are down to zero. Some experience joy today, but tomorrow, they are suffering from depression. God does not heal, and then there is a reversal. When he does a thing, it is permanent. Nothing can change it. When he heals, it is complete, whole. He does not heal one area and leave the other unattended. That is not God. He heals like no one can.

His Will Is Ever Done on Earth

Concerning his children, God's will must be done. The word of God says he rules in the affairs of men.

The will of the devil can never triumph over the child of God. Whatever may happen, what God says concerning his children is what will be done. The devil and his hosts must lose. The person who belongs to God cannot be subject to the will of the wicked ones of this world. If the enemies try, they will fail. The Bible says the rod of the wicked shall not rest on the land allotted to the righteous forever.

If the enemy makes an effort over the life of his children, God thwarts it and thereby glorifies himself. Nothing that does not bring glory to God can remain forever in the life of his children when he is in charge. No matter what happens, he sees to it that his will regarding every aspect of the life of the believer is done.

He Advocates for Us

An appearance in court is not complete without a lawyer. We have no greater advocate than the Lord Jesus. The Bible says he intercedes for us with the father. He speaks for us where we do not have a voice. He uses people to speak in our favor where we have no one. It is a real issue when a human being has no one to speak in his or her favor. For instance, someone must speak in a person's favor before he or she gets chosen over others in a bid for a job in a company. Someone must be in a position to advocate on our behalf where good things are being shared. It is normal since we cannot be everywhere. The reason many lack certain things is that no one recommends them or speaks well on their behalf. God does this best.

Where his children are not, God raises people to advocate for them. In the palace of Pharaoh, God raised a voice for Joseph. This was a young man who had been forgotten in prison. The man who threw him in prison did not bother to check how he was doing. Joseph was in prison, but there was no specific time he was to spend there. He had no hope of ever coming out again. The servant of Pharaoh did not remember Joseph anymore. But that was until the day God stepped into his matter and raised an advocate for him to speak to the king.

He Avenges for Us

The Bible says vengeance belongs to God. His word says his children should let him carry out vengeance on their behalf. He is the God who avenges his children on their enemies in such a way that the children do not need to break a sweat. When he avenges, it is comprehensive. It is complete.

The children of Israel were exploited for several generations in Egypt. They got to the edge of the Red Sea, and their enemies still came after them. They cried to God, and he stepped in for them. He wrought a vengeance that was both complete and permanent.

THE BENEFITS WE
HAVE IN CHRIST

God gives assignments and gives us rewards when we get them done. He instructs, and he rewards when we follow his instructions. God does not ask us to do what he knows is impossible for us to do. When he says we should do a thing, he is right there waiting to assist us to get it done. Actually, all instructions that God gives are for our benefit. He gives them because he knows we will profit from them.

At the baptism of Christ by John, God said we should hear Jesus. He knows when we do we have much to gain. God is in the business of conferring benefits. Like the earthly father, he gives rewards because he is our father. No child enjoys a father who does not return home with goodies for his children. No child will feel loved when the father does not give him or her gifts, sometimes impromptu. There are so many passages in the Bible where God is compared to a father. In fact, he calls himself our father—that is, the father of those who trust in him.

He says like any earthly father, he gives good things to his children (Mathew 7:8–11):

> For every one that asketh receiveth; and he that seeketh findeth; and to him that knocketh it shall be opened. Or what man is there of you, whom if his son ask bread, will he give him a stone? Or if he ask a fish, will he give him a serpent? If ye then, being evil, know how to give good gifts unto your children, how much more

shall your Father which is in heaven give good things
to them that ask him?

As a father does, God says we should ask and he will give (Matthew
7:7–8): "Ask, and it shall be given you; seek, and ye shall find; knock,
and it shall be opened unto you: For every one that asketh receiveth; and
he that seeketh findeth; and to him that knocketh it shall be opened."

He says we should not despise him; rather, we should honor him as
a father (Malachi 1:6);

A son honoureth his father, and a servant his master:
if then I be a father, where is mine honour? and if I
be a master, where is my fear? saith the Lord of hosts
unto you, O priests, that despise my name. And ye say,
Wherein have we despised thy name?

He is our father. As his children, some of the benefits God has for
us are as follows:

He Gives the Joy of Salvation

The joy of salvation is the most important of benefits for us to have
from God. For our salvation was the main purpose for which the Lord
Jesus came into the world. When we have him in our lives, we have all.
In fact, salvation is the foundation for any other thing God does in our
lives. Salvation is the door of access to his other benefits. For this reason,
Jesus says in Matthew 6:33, "But seek ye first the kingdom of God, and
his righteousness; and all these things shall be added unto you."

The truth is that when we have salvation, we have all. Jesus says all
other things shall follow. Salvation is where we should focus. We should
ensure we settle that aspect if we would walk with God, if we would
expect anything from him. There is no sitting on the wall about this.
There is no halfway. There is no room for one leg in, one leg out. We
cannot afford to be lukewarm.

Actually, one reason many do not get incremental, noticeable
progress in their relationship with God may be because they have yet

to resolve their salvation. They are not consistent in the relationship they believe they have with God. When this relationship is settled and it is consistent, the story of a believer should be like a good car that travels toward a destination. It goes forward, never backward. It goes consistently. With every mile it covers, it gets closer to the destination. Every day a believer is in the Lord, he or she should have testimony of God's goodness, kindness, love, protection, and provision. When believers walk with God, they have in their hearts the joy of salvation. The joy of salvation continuously fills the heart of believers, and this strengthens them to continue the journey until that final day when they receive the crown in glory. Whatever is different from this means the believer needs to check his or her relationship with God.

What the Joy of Salvation Does in the Life of the Believer

It gives comfort. When the relationship is right, God fills our heart with the joy of his salvation. No matter what we may be passing through, the joy envelopes us and gives us comfort. The experiences of God's mercy that we have every day—his kindness, his provision, his protection—imbue us with confidence that no matter what happens, God is in charge. The joy of salvation makes us know that no matter how much the enemy tries, God will give us victory ultimately.

It rekindles hope. The joy of salvation rekindles hope in the believer. This is important because it is hope that keeps all humans going. Hope of a day when freedom would come kept the children of Israel going in Egypt, the land of their bondage. The hope that God would surely set them free from their oppressors kept them calling on God. Hope that rain will fall and it will grow again is all that the stump of a tree has. The Bible says at the smell of water, what has been made stump comes alive and grows again.

Hope is alive and is rekindled when one has the joy of salvation. The Holy Spirit reminds the believer that for as long as we are alive, God is able to do what he has promised to do. For as long as we remain in him, our expectations shall not be cut off.

It opens the door to more joy. Joy is the currency by which we can attract more joy. When we rejoice always in our God, he adds to us more reasons to rejoice. When we rejoice, we give praise to God. When we rejoice in the Lord, we thank him all the time. When we rejoice, we give him glory for what he has done and that which he shall yet do. The believer who does this opens the door for more joy. The joy of salvation makes us rejoice always.

It gives us courage. The joy of salvation gives one courage to forge ahead. We need courage to face many of life's challenges. Without it, many give up. That is why there are so many stories of suicide around. It is because people lose courage. The joy of salvation gives the kind of courage that the person who is not saved may not have. God's courage is different from any other. The courage God puts in us ensures we remain committed when others grumble about God. It is because he makes us see what others do not see. The person in whom there is God's kind of courage wants to confront challenges even when others think it is foolishness to do so. God's kind of courage was exhibited by Joshua and Caleb at a time when others were discouraged.

It makes the heart a ready ground for the Holy Spirit to impart. The joy of salvation makes the believer a ground where Holy Spirit is able to impart at all times. The heart without joy shuts the Holy Spirit out. But when we rejoice in the Lord always, his spirit has a constant atmosphere where he gives instructions, leads, comforts, instructs, corrects, and so on. The believer needs the Holy Spirit. Without him, the race cannot be as smooth as it should be for the child of God. The joy of salvation provides the right atmosphere for the spirit of God to operate in.

It helps us fulfil our God-given dream. All that God purposes to do in the life of his children, he settled it before we were born. Fulfilling it while we are on earth is what is left. Whether or not people fulfil what God has purposed for them remains their choice, not God's. When a person fulfils what God purposed for him or her, it means a process that began before creation is being completed. For all manner of reasons, many are leaving the earth without completing the process. The blame is never God's but that of the person he has created and imbued with a purpose.

This is the reason it is important we take the message of salvation seriously and walk accordingly. When a person confronts obstacles in the effort to fulfill his or her God-given dream but is not in God, the obstacle remains unmoved and immovable. For it is only in the name of Jesus that obstacles are overcome. It happens only with the help of God. One could imagine what would have happened to the children of Israel if they had not called on God in Egypt. One could imagine what would have happened to Joseph and his dream in Egypt, if he had not remained faithful and fully committed to God. Many people refuse to cry to God in their distress. They refuse to acknowledge the God of all flesh. In fact, they say there is no God. The Bible says in the book of Psalms that the fool says in his heart that there is no God.

One could imagine what would have happened if at the time God sent Moses to the children of Israel in Egypt, they had rejected him. Many are rejecting their Moses, the prophet God sends to deliver and help them fulfill their God-given dreams. One could imagine what would have happened if the children of Israel had ignored God at the time he gave instructions that they should kill a lamb and put the blood on their doorposts. That was the night uncountable children of Egypt were slaughtered in the course of the night. The lamb killed by the Israelites foreshadowed Jesus, whom John the Baptist called the lamb of God—the lamb of God who takes away the sins of the world. Many are losing what they should keep; they are losing their lives because they ignore the call made by God that all should come to him through his son, Jesus.

The chances of a person failing to fulfill his or her God-given dream or destiny began with the first man, Adam. From the time mankind sinned, there has been no 100 percent guarantee that a person will fulfill his or her destiny. Sin is one reason. The wickedness of man to man is another. The chances have been reduced to fifty-fifty, and it is made worse when enemies simply decide to constitute themselves as obstacles in the path of a person. It happens. When Adam sinned, he aborted the implantation to do all that God ordained man to do on earth—live in dominion, dwell in peace, multiply, rule, and so on.

The servant of God Myles Monroe explains it this way:

When Adam broke God's law, he aborted his seed's potential for becoming all they were intended to be. Men and women throughout all ages have fallen far short of the glory of the Creator. The word glory means the "true nature" or "full essence" of a thing. In other words, to fall short of glory means to live below your true potential. This is what God calls sin. Sin is not a behavior; it is a disposition.

All men are born sinners. All men are sinners. As the first man lost that chance, so it takes Jesus to regain the chance. Therefore, Jesus is the embodiment of God's second chance, the embodiment of God's redemption, of salvation, of regaining the opportunity to be what God says man should be, as noted in Romans 5:12, 17;

> Therefore, just as sin entered the world through one man, and death through sin, and in this way death came to all men, because all sinned [in Adam] ... Consequently, just as the result of one trespass was condemnation for all men, so also the result of one act of righteousness was justification that brings life for all men. For if by one man's offence death reigned by one; much more they which receive abundance of grace and of the gift of righteousness shall reign in life by one, Jesus Christ.

Until a person has Jesus, he or she is not complete. For as Munroe puts it, "You come to the awareness that understanding and releasing your potential is simply becoming yourself as God our Creator originally intended." It is not just prospering in physical or financial terms that we have in mind here. It is prospering on earth and also making it to heaven. It takes Jesus to achieve both, as he is the way, the truth, and the life.

Without Jesus, a person may be seen to have prospered on earth in materials things, but he loses his soul. The Bible asks what profit anyone has when he or she gains the whole world but loses his or her soul. Perhaps it is important we get the understanding that while there is a purpose for which God sent people to earth, they may pass through the earth without fulfilling their God-propelled purpose or their God-given dream. It happens to many, and it speaks to a lack of completeness that only God makes possible in the lives of those who surrender to him.

In this regard, Munroe gives a succinct explanation:

> The purpose of a thing is the original intent or desire of the one who created it. Thus, the purpose of a thing cannot be known by asking anyone other than the designer or the manufacturer. If we entered the laboratory of an inventor and you asked me what a certain contraption was supposed to do, I might guess at what service or function it could perform, but only the inventor would be able to confirm or reject my suggestion. The purpose of a thing cannot be known by asking anyone other than the designer or the manufacturer. Likewise, the ability of that product to fulfill its purpose is designed into the product.
>
> No manufacturer would suggest that you use his appliance to wash clothes unless he intended for it to wash clothes. If I assume that the machine is a clothes dryer and complain to the dealer that the machine won't dry my clothes, the manufacturer will most certainly respond, "But that machine isn't supposed to dry clothes. Use it to wash clothes and it'll work fine. But don't ask it to dry clothes, because it can't. I didn't build it to dry clothes." The manufacturer determines both the product's purpose and how it will function to fulfill that purpose.

He Wires Us for Exploits

The believer is wired to do exploits. We are an embodiment of great things waiting to happen. It is how God has purposed it. God puts into his children the grace to do exploits. This is a grace imparted by the anointing at the point when we surrender our lives to Jesus. It is one aspect of a complete package that becomes manifest as we grow in him. As we do, there is an incremental surge in the level of this grace in our lives, such that the gift and the calling of each person become manifest, and they operate effectively in that office. This is a benefit that only the children of God can boast of. In this, we have great leaders and teachers of the word with uncommon insight and revelations—pastors, evangelists, prophets, and apostles.

God has said what his children will be in Deuteronomy 28:1–10:

> And it shall come to pass, if thou shalt hearken diligently unto the voice of the LORD thy God, to observe and to do all his commandments which I command thee this day, that the LORD thy God will set thee on high above all nations of the earth: And all these blessings shall come on thee, and overtake thee, if thou shalt hearken unto the voice of the LORD thy God. Blessed shalt thou be in the city, and blessed shalt thou be in the field. Blessed shall be the fruit of thy body, and the fruit of thy ground, and the fruit of thy cattle, the increase of thy kine, and the flocks of thy sheep. Blessed shall be thy basket and thy store. Blessed shalt thou be when thou comest in, and blessed shalt thou be when thou goest out. The LORD shall cause thine enemies that rise up against thee to be smitten before thy face: they shall come out against thee one way, and flee before thee seven ways. The LORD shall command the blessing upon thee in thy storehouses, and in all that thou settest thine hand unto; and he shall bless thee in the land which the LORD thy God giveth thee. The LORD shall establish thee an holy people unto himself, as he hath sworn unto thee, if thou shalt keep the commandments of the LORD thy God, and walk in his ways. And all people of the earth shall see that thou art called by the name of the LORD; and they shall be afraid of thee.

Here are some of God's blessings, his promises that are enumerated for all his children. Who can embody and manifest all of these and not leave a mark in generations born and unborn? In God's words is the grace to do exploits that he has released upon those who are his. We have examples in the Bible of people concerning whom God made promises. They did exploits in the course of their stay on this earth.

Samson

This was a man God spoke to his parents about even before he was conceived. The promises are in Judges 13:2–5:

> And there was a certain man of Zorah, of the family of the Danites, whose name was Manoah; and his wife was barren, and bare not. And the angel of the LORD appeared unto the woman, and said unto her, Behold now, thou art barren, and bearest not: but thou shalt conceive, and bear a son. Now therefore beware, I pray thee, and drink not wine nor strong drink, and eat not any unclean thing: For, lo, thou shalt conceive, and bear a son; and no razor shall come on his head: for the child shall be a Nazarite unto God from the womb: and he shall begin to deliver Israel out of the hand of the Philistines.

One must consider that Samson was filled with the Holy Spirit from the womb. He was born with the spirit of God highly active in him to make him do that which God said he would do. He was wired to do exploits. Actually all that Samson did was not because of his physical powers but as a result of the Holy Spirit who manifested powerfully in him. When the Holy Spirit was in operation in him, Samson was not a normal human being. For God was the one operating in him and through him.

This is the way God has programmed believers who have Jesus in their life. They are helped by God's spirit to do exploits. Without Jesus, no man can. With him in us, nothing shall be impossible. For Samson, nothing was impossible. No number of soldiers was too large for him to take on, because the Spirit of God was in operation.

Samuel

Samuel the prophet was the product of prayer. He was the outcome of the word of blessing pronounced by the priest of God, Eli. As a child, he did not know who the God of Israel was until God revealed himself to him. What God said to him came to pass on the house of Eli, and Samuel increasingly grew to become what was purposed for him as noted in 1 Samuel 3:19-20: "And Samuel grew, and the LORD was with him, and did let none of his words fall to the ground. And all Israel from Dan even to Beersheba knew that Samuel was established to be a prophet of the LORD."

What Samuel manifested was what God designed him for. He was wired to be the leader of the nation, the judge to the people, the priest of the most high God, the kingmaker.

John the Baptist

Like Samson, John was a product of a prophecy. His father, Zacharias, was a priest, doing his duty in the temple when God sent his angel to reveal his plan in Luke 1:13–19:

> But the angel said unto him, Fear not, Zacharias: for thy prayer is heard; and thy wife Elisabeth shall bear thee a son, and thou shalt call his name John. And thou shalt have joy and gladness; and many shall rejoice at his birth. For he shall be great in the sight of the Lord, and shall drink neither wine nor strong drink; and he shall be filled with the Holy Ghost, even from his mother's womb. And many of the children of Israel shall he turn to the Lord their God. And he shall go before him in the spirit and power of Elias, to turn the hearts of the fathers to the children, and the disobedient to the wisdom of the just; to make ready a people prepared for the Lord. And Zacharias said unto the angel, Whereby

shall I know this? for I am an old man, and my wife well
stricken in years. And the angel answering said unto
him, I am Gabriel, that stand in the presence of God;
and am sent to speak unto thee.

John carried the anointing of God right from the womb as he was
purposely sent for an assignment. Every believer has an assignment.
When we know exactly what it is and we walk in it, then we have
opened up ourselves for what only God can do. The person in whom
and through whom God carries out his plan will no doubt be an
instrument for exploits. In him, God will do that which only he can do.

He Configures Us to Rule

From creation, God configured man to rule. Man is the masterpiece
of his creation. Man is loaded to be God's representation on the earth.
He made man God on the earth. God's plan for man is for kingship
and rulership. Man is not made for suffering, disease, and death. Man
was made for bliss and foreverness. Sin came in to shatter this plan,
but Christ came in with the package of redemption. As the Bibles says
in Romans 6:23, "For the wages of sin is death; but the gift of God is
eternal life through Jesus Christ our Lord."

The life of a man is anchored around what God has designed for
him to do. Man having missed it in the garden of Eden, it takes God's
light, instruction, and direction to get us to actually function as we are
designed. When we are in him, we have dominion. We have power
and authority over all that is in creation. We rule, we are not ruled. We
determine what happens on earth, not that others do over us. When
we adjust to the divine mandate for our lives, nothing can stop us.
But making this adjustment takes understanding, a reason this book
is in your hand. For it is understanding that brings about outstanding
performance. As children of God, we are configured to rule. For we
are endowed by his grace to rule.

THE ROLE OF THE BELIEVER

There is a role for us to play in God's plan for humans. This is because each party in a relationship has his or her duties and obligations. Each has a role; otherwise, there can be no relationship. In the God-human relationship, we have a role. God has prepared all things. He is willing and ready to receive us unto himself and do what only he can do in our lives. But we must be willing to play our part.

The angle to the relationship that many miss is that God plays his part; he cannot play ours for us. He can give us the grace to play the part that is ours. He can help us along with it. But he will not take on our role for us. Why? He is God. We are humans, made of flesh and spirit. God is spirit. In the earthly terrestrial, there is what he has ordained for humans to do. He is a God of principle. He has arranged the God-human relationship based on principle. He does not break his principle, definitely not for humans who fail to do their bit. If any person turns his back to him, God would let him or her be. He does not compel anyone. Maybe this is difficult to digest. But it is the truth. We can use Biblical examples to establish this narrative.

In the relationship God established with Adam in the garden at Eden, we see God create the heaven and the earth. He placed man in the garden. He descended from heaven in the cool of the day to fellowship with man. That was his part. He played it. He gave man a role to tend the garden, and he expected Adam to fellowship with him.

He also issued an instruction. For as long as man continued walk in this instruction, all was well. It meant both sides abided by the allotted respective roles in the relationship. When he arrived in the garden one day and found that man had stepped out of the relationship through disobedience, things went the other way. These days, many overlook this strict arrangement, even though they say they worship God. They are not willing to do what God says, but they expect God to do his bit. This thing does not work that way. The going may be tough. Temptations will come. There will be stress. There will be moments when the load seems too heavy. Yet we have to continue, trusting that God will help. We are made to understand that God does not give an assignment for which he has not released the grace to accomplish. God does not give instruction that he knows we will be unable to fulfil.

When he instructs, he stands there ready to also help get it done. He is ready to release grace. He can help our faith. He can give comfort. He gives succor. He makes a way where there is no way. Maybe we should ask why Jesus said he would send the comforter as he promised. He knows there will be moments when we will need the Holy Spirit to help us carry on with the role God has assigned to us. Why did the Bible say we should ask? It is because there will be moments when we will need his help in the course of the journey.

Why is it that Moses said he and the children of Israel would not want to embark on the journey to the Promised Land except God was present with them? He knew that while carrying out the instruction God gave, there would be obstacles, yet the role assigned to them as humans must be fulfilled. God did not decide to pick the children of Israel and drop them in Canaan. He could do it. But he did not. He wanted them to go through the journey. In the process, he strengthened them. God made them realize they could not do anything on their own except he helped them. The children of Israel played their part by embarking, as God had instructed them, on a journey they knew would be tough. If they had stayed back in Egypt, the Promised Land would have eluded them.

We must not hang back from the role God expects us to play. It is the only way he will do what he has promised to do. He steps in and completes that which only he can when we do what he says we should do.

At the time we heed the call of the King as his children, we accept that we are ready to be made complete in Christ the Savior. As such, we need to pay attention to the following:

Be Willing to Obey

The God-human relationship is one of obedience all the way. Obedience is the key. God places much emphasis on it in the Bible. There is one such verse in Isaiah 1:19: "If ye be willing and obedient, ye shall eat the good of the land."

There is a warning regarding this in 1 Samuel 15:22: "And Samuel said, Hath the Lord as great delight in burnt offerings and sacrifices, as in obeying the voice of the Lord? Behold, to obey is better than sacrifice, and to hearken than the fat of rams."

Jesus is the way; he knows the way. He knows the end from the beginning. When we obey him, we cannot miss it. The journey is fraught with issues. It takes God to navigate them successfully. With each step taken, it is important that we listen to his instruction for the next step to take. Nothing can be taken for granted. He knows what we do not know. He knows better than we do, and it is the reason he says we shall hear his voice telling us this is the way, follow it.

It is in the area of obedience that many get it wrong. Once they do, every other thing in the relationship is affected. We often get to a point we feel we know the right things to do, so we do what we think is right without asking God for his guidance. But God wants to lead always. He wants to instruct. He knows best. What we think is the best may not be his plan for us. Many have made this mistake and missed their destiny. They settle for less than God has planned for them. Obedience is the key to the relationship with God. It is not for nothing Jesus says he is the good shepherd. He says he calls and his own hear him. This speaks to obedience. God calls always. Do we hear him and obey?

He calls all the time to his sheep so that we do not go astray. But do we listen? Listen to God. Be willing to obey him all the way. It is the key that opens all the doors in the God–human relationship.

Take Him at His Word

God's word is not just the letter we see in the Bible. It is spirit. Jesus provides clarification in John 6:63: "It is the spirit that quickeneth; the flesh profiteth nothing: the words that I speak unto you, they are spirit, and they are life."

The Bible says of the word of God in Hebrews 4:12: "For the word of God is quick, and powerful, and sharper than any twoedged sword, piercing even to the dividing asunder of soul and spirit, and of the joints and marrow, and is a discerner of the thoughts and intents of the heart."

When we take what God says, and we believe it as he has said it, we are in for a great harvest. In his word is his promise. In believing his promise is our reward as his children.

Tell Him What He Says

God will not deny his word. In fact, God takes what he says as binding upon him. It must be the reason he swore by himself and said in blessing he would bless Abraham.

God's word is for every situation we may find ourselves in. Whatever the issues are, all we need is to locate the word of God that addresses it. There is no human condition, problem, or obstacle that the word of God does not address. There is something God must have said he will do regarding that situation that seems so stifling, so peculiar. He has his word for prosperity. He has words in regard to the single or unmarried person. He has a word for the widow and for the barren, for deliverance from enemies, for child-bearing, and so on.

The power of the promise is greater than the power of the problem. The dynamics of your attainment is packaged in God's promise. Tell God what he says concerning your specific situation, and he will honor his word.

Get into the Class of God

Get into God's class, and see things as God sees them. It is your responsibility to so do, not God's. The time he wanted to be man and he came down to earth, he had already done so. Now it is for us to draw to him and aspire to what he expects us to be in thought, in word, and in action. For God says as he is, so we are, according to 1 John 4:17: "Herein is our love made perfect, that we may have boldness in the day of judgment: because as he is, so are we in this world."

We have to do this because it is then we begin to see things the way he sees them. We cannot remain in the carnal state and be in the class of God. We cannot see what he sees if we continue to see things only by sight and not by faith. God does not see us as mere humans. He sees differently. With his spirit in us, we are in a different class, in his class. And that is where we should be. His word says in John 1:12, "But as many as received him, to them gave he power to become the sons of God, even to them that believe on his name."

The first birth makes every human being a loser. The second birth makes God's children winners. There will be carnal people, people who operate in the flesh. But God's children are in a different class. Regarding his children, whose bodies are the temple of the Holy Spirit, he says in Psalm 82:6, "I have said, Ye are gods; and all of you are children of the most High."

The way to be what he wants us to be is to move upward to his class. It is then we get access into his thought and get to know what he has in mind for us. Our God is of a different class, and he says so in Isaiah 55:8–11:

> For my thoughts are not your thoughts, neither are your ways my ways, saith the LORD. For as the heavens are higher than the earth, so are my ways higher than your ways, and my thoughts than your thoughts. For as the rain cometh down, and the snow from heaven, and returneth not thither, but watereth the earth, and maketh it bring forth and bud, that it may give seed to the sower, and bread to the eater: So shall my word be

that goeth forth out of my mouth: it shall not return unto me void, but it shall accomplish that which I please, and it shall prosper in the thing whereto I sent it.

Be Fully Persuaded

Be persuaded that the God we serve is able to attend to all issues no matter what they are. The Bible asks us to so do in Romans 4:21: "And being fully persuaded that, what he had promised, he was able also to perform."

God attaches importance to this. He says no one who is not fully persuaded will get anything from him in James 1:5–8:

> If any of you lack wisdom, let him ask of God, that giveth to all men liberally, and upbraideth not; and it shall be given him. But let him ask in faith, nothing wavering. For he that wavereth is like a wave of the sea driven with the wind and tossed. For let not that man think that he shall receive any thing of the Lord. A double minded man is unstable in all his ways.

It is the person who is fully persuaded who continues to ask without looking back, no matter what happens. Ask, and be fully persuaded that you will receive.

This requires that we are focused on Jesus always. Never look away. Never look back. Never turn to look at what are called facts. Leave the data alone, and focus your attention on God. He is more than the data. He can do what the data cannot do. This is the God who does to the supernatural what no man or scientist can do. Peter wanted to walk on the sea like Jesus, and when Jesus gave the instruction, he did walk on the sea. He did not sink for as long as he focused on Jesus. When he lost focus, he began to sink. He took his eyes away from Jesus. Whatever the storm may be, never look away from the author and finisher of our faith. Do not be distracted. Be fully persuaded that he will do what he says he will do, and focus on him.

Flow in Wisdom and Revelation

Wisdom guides, just as revelation is a lamp that shows the way. Both are needed if the walk with God is to continue. The Bible recommends it according to Ephesians 1:17–23;

> That the God of our Lord Jesus Christ, the Father of glory, may give unto you the spirit of wisdom and revelation in the knowledge of him: The eyes of your understanding being enlightened; that ye may know what is the hope of his calling, and what the riches of the glory of his inheritance in the saints.

When a man has the wisdom of God, he walks and thinks on the same plane as God thinks. He sees as God sees. God does not focus on the moment. He never focuses on those challenges confronting the believer. Rather he looks into the future; he uses the present situation the believer finds him- or herself in to launch that person into the glorious future he has prepared. This is as true for the final glorification in heaven as it is for the journey of the believer on earth. It is the reason the Bible says in Ephesians 1:17–23,

> That the God of our Lord Jesus Christ, the Father of glory, may give unto you the spirit of wisdom and revelation in the knowledge of him: The eyes of your understanding being enlightened; that ye may know what is the hope of his calling, and what the riches of the glory of his inheritance in the saints, And what is the exceeding greatness of his power to us-ward who believe, according to the working of his mighty power, Which he wrought in Christ, when he raised him from the dead, and set him at his own right hand in the heavenly places, Far above all principality, and power, and might, and dominion, and every name that is named, not only in this world, but also in that which is to come: And hath put all things under his feet, and

gave him to be the head over all things to the church,
Which is his body, the fulness of him that filleth all
in all.

The believer needs the wisdom, revelation and the understanding
that comes from God in order to continue the journey. Without them,
it is easy to fall back and miss out on what God has prepared here and
in the hereafter. Wisdom and revelation are spirits; the believer needs
to ask for them, as well as walk in them. That is the way to remain at
his feet and benefit from what only he can do.

In God's arrangement, the gateway to greatness is by wisdom and
revelation. Key into it.

Never Be Discouraged

We must not let challenges discourage us. We must not give up.
Actually, it is what the enemy wants to see. For the battle the devil
wages against the children of God is essentially in the mind. Once the
mind remains steadfast on the Lord, the battle is practically won. There
is nothing the devil can do, for eventually victory that only God gives
becomes manifest.

There are many in the faith who have demonstrated what it means
to be confronted with challenges and refuse to be discouraged. There
was famine in the land. Isaac was instructed by God to stay where he
was. He did. The Bible says in Genesis 26:12, "Then Isaac sowed in
that land, and received in the same year an hundredfold: and the Lord
blessed him."

He did not let the fact of the famine to discourage him. He sowed,
and he reaped. Situations that discourage should not be the reason we
turn away from God or disobey him. When we refuse to be discouraged,
we will reap the benefits God has set aside for us.

David lost all he had to invaders, but he encouraged himself. Jabez
did not let the size of his challenge discourage him. A close look at what
the issues regarding Jabez were would give one an idea of how much
of a load he needed to have removed from his life. He was extremely

poor. He was a man who knew nothing but sorrow. His name meant sorrow. Had he concentrated on his situation rather than look up to God, he would have been discouraged. He came to God and cried for help, rather than lament about his problems and get discouraged.

Job was not discouraged. This was a man who was down, completely. But his case is a reason every believer should bear in mind what is stated in Micah 7:8; "Rejoice not against me, O mine enemy: when I fall, I shall arise; when I sit in darkness, the LORD shall be a light unto me."

When those moments come when one wants to be discouraged, that is the moment to remember Psalm 3:2–3; "Many there be which say of my soul, There is no help for him in God. But thou, O LORD, art a shield for me; my glory, and the lifter up of mine head."

No matter what happens as a child of God, no matter what we go through, the mind should be in us what is stated in Romans 8:28, 37; "And we know that all things work together for good to them that love God, to them who are the called according to his purpose. Nay, in all these things we are more than conquerors through him that loved us."

The Bible equally has a word of caution in 2 Corinthians 4:1: "Therefore seeing we have this ministry, as we have received mercy, we faint not."

Invest in Greatness

No one gains great things in life without investing in a cause. Peter and the rest of the disciples left all and followed Jesus. They were investing in greatness. These were unlettered men, but they became greater many of the lettered and important people of their time. These men gave up all and did something others would not do. At one stage, the implication of what he had done seemed to hit Peter, so he asked questions of Jesus in Mark 10:28–31:

> Then Peter began to say unto him, Lo, we have left all, and have followed thee. And Jesus answered and said, Verily I say unto you, There is no man that hath left house, or brethren, or sisters, or father, or mother,

or wife, or children, or lands, for my sake, and the gospel's, But he shall receive an hundredfold now in this time, houses, and brethren, and sisters, and mothers, and children, and lands, with persecutions; and in the world to come eternal life. But many that are first shall be last; and the last first.

Invest in the kingdom, and get in return the kind of dividends only the kingdom can give. There can be no returns without an initial investment.